HEAD FIRST

HEAD FIRST

a crash course in positivity

Casey—
I hope my story
and what I've learned
will help you along your
journey!

Steve H. Lawton

Fedd Books
P.O. Box 341973
Austin, TX 78734
www.thefeddagency.com

Published in association with The Fedd Agency, Inc., a literary agency.

ISBN: 978-1-943217-32-8
eISBN: 978-1-943217-33-5

Printed in the United States of America

First Edition 15 14 13 10 09 / 10 9 8 7 6 5 4 3 2

To Deanna.

Without you, I wouldn't be who I am today,
I wouldn't be here at all, and this book would not exist.
Thank you for being my partner and the love of my life.

CONTENTS

Prologue

For as long as I can remember, I have loved skiing.

I was hooked when I skied for the first time at Heavenly Resort in Lake Tahoe, California, at five years old. My parents have an 8mm film of my first day, and the ear-to-ear grin on my face says it all. I love the feeling of attacking a bump run or cruising down a perfectly groomed slope on a pristine morning with the sun shining and the brisk mountain air stinging my face. It was on one of these perfect mornings in March 2014 at Breckenridge, Colorado, when this love story turned into a tragedy.

There were eight of us on this spring break ski trip: my family of four including Deanna, my wife of twenty-four years, our son Ryan (17), and our daughter Katie (15), as well as my wife's sister Dana Markes, her husband Peter, and their kids, Colin (17) and Courtney (16). Our families have grown together in the same neighborhood and our children are more like siblings than cousins.

On the second day of our trip, Peter (a skier arguably good enough to be on a Warren Miller video) and I decided to hit the lifts with Ryan and Colin as soon as they opened. We wanted to get in a few challenging runs before our wives and daughters joined us because they did not like the expert runs that Peter and I enjoyed. At the top of Peak 8 our sons decided to ski on the terrain park trails while Peter and I chose the runs under the 6-Chair lift where we could ski some of the most challenging slopes on the mountain. Before heading down I called Deanna to let her know where we would be, and at 8:58 a.m. I turned on my "SkiTracks"—a phone app that monitors where you ski, your speed, and elevation changes. That was the last thing I remember for most of the next five days. The events that follow have been pieced together from what Peter and my family have related, reports from the ski patrol and medical centers, and the information collected by my SkiTracks app.

Peter and I reached the top of the 6-Chair lift, which is at an elevation of approximately 10,000 feet, just before 9:15 a.m. We were among the first people on the slopes that morning, and the conditions were PERFECT. Six feet of snow base, fresh snow within the last twenty-four hours, clear skies, no wind, and temperatures comfortably below freezing. If you are a skier, you will be with me in recognizing this as our happy place.

Peter asked if I wanted to do a mogul (a bump run) or a groomed run (a trail that has been smoothed out) first, and I decided since it was our first run of the day it would be better to warm-up on a groomed run. We started down the only groomed option from that chair lift, which was a steep black diamond run (an expert level slope). It was aptly named Amen Run. I started down the run first, and Peter waited at the top, allowing me to get a head start. We were both almost giddy at that great moment.

However, that first run of the day didn't go as planned. I was a few hundred yards down the run when Peter heard me yell, "Whoa!" He looked up, saw me come out of my skis in the center of the run, fly through the air, land on my back with a thud, and continue sliding headfirst, accelerating down the steep, freshly-groomed slope. Because the run was so steep, Peter stopped watching me to concentrate on his skiing to get down the hill to retrieve my skis and poles. When he came across the skis, he thought, *That's strange—they are sitting side by side as if he placed them here to put them on.* In all my years of skiing, I've never seen a fall where someone fell and left their skis behind so perfectly aligned.

Peter picked up my skis, looked around for me, and I was nowhere to be seen. He called out my name, and there was no reply. He couldn't see me from the run, but he could see the path my body made down the freshly groomed trail, so he followed it. A hundred yards down the mountain the run veered left, but my path continued straight toward a lone, large pine tree just off the run. Peter began to panic when he realized something was terribly wrong. It wasn't until he was nearly at the tree that I was visible, and what he saw was horrifying.

I was unconscious, my torso wrapped around the trunk of the tree. The back of my helmet was crushed and I was bleeding from the back of my head, nose, ears, and mouth. We would find out later that my SkiTracks app recorded my speed when I hit the tree at a terrifying 45 mph. The nightmare unfolding before us was just about the worst possible outcome to what we thought was going to be a perfect day.

Everything that happened after that moment, from the decisions made and actions taken in the first few minutes, to my attitude and hard work in the days and months ahead led to a miraculous recovery.

This story is not about the accident; it's about the recovery and the importance of a positive attitude. It's about how our attitude can affect our outcomes and includes practical ways for all of us to improve our attitude and our outcomes.

Introduction

The fact that you have this book in your hands is amazing. My story is crazy, and it's a miracle that I survived and recovered well enough to share it with you. I honestly feel I'm a walking miracle and God brought me back for a purpose—to share my story and what I learned about positivity.

It all started with that skiing accident in the spring of 2014. The doctors weren't sure I would survive. I had a multitude of severe injuries to my head, chest, neck, and back. Even though many of them could have killed me or caused permanent damage, I recovered. And amazingly, I did it far faster and far more completely than the doctors ever expected. To simply survive was remarkable—to recover was miraculous.

Even when you are in situations where being positive or happy is unimaginable, can you still benefit from positivity? The short answer is yes. I know because a positive attitude literally saved my life.

I have always been positive, and thankfully I built up what psychologists call a "positivity offset" before the accident. As it turns out, that trait was crucial for me to survive and recover. Both my wife and I are naturally positive people, and we simply brought that attitude into the situation without forcing it. About a year after the accident, as my recovery was coming to a close, I realized the importance of a positive attitude and how critical of a role it played in my recovery.

As I started sharing my story with my family, friends, and coworkers, the aspects of positivity that saved my life have crystalized into eight pragmatic principles anyone can adopt. This book tells my story accompanied by those principles. As I thought about my story, I realized that it isn't the accident that makes it powerful; it's the recovery. I know that a positive attitude saved my life, led me down the road to recovery, and is a powerful example of how attitudes affect outcomes. Numerous scientific studies have proven the link between attitudes and outcomes. Positivity not only makes you happier; it also makes your life more fulfilling, improves your health, cultivates better relationships, improves outcomes at work, changes the course of your career, and even enables large groups or companies to achieve better results.

Not only will the positivity principles in this book help improve your mindset and increase the likelihood of a good outcome in any given moment, they will also build up your overall positivity that will benefit you in times of stress. In psychology literature, it's called a positivity offset. I like to think of it as fitness for your attitude. Just like physical fitness, when you work out regularly, not only do you get the benefits of having a lot of energy and feeling good while you are in shape, if you suffer an injury or a health crisis, your fitness will help you recover faster. It's the same for positivity. If you practice positivity on a regular basis, you will increase your "attitude fitness." You will literally change the neuron connections and circuits in your brain and become more positive and optimistic. This physical change that takes place in our brains happens through a concept that doctors and scientists call neuroplasticity. And it is constantly at work in all of us. Through neuroplasticity, we get better at what we practice because our brain is rewiring itself to make it easier to do that activity. It works for physical activities, like practicing golf or tennis, and it works for thinking activities in the same way. When you practice positivity, not only will you get the scientifically proven benefits of positivity at the moment, you will also be able to use your higher positivity offset to overcome an obstacle that comes your way.

How many obstacles, challenges, and setbacks have you already overcome in your life? For most of us, it's a lot. We've all had them—from problems at work, financial challenges, a disagreement with a spouse or loved one, behavioral difficulties with a child, an injury, a frightening diagnosis, or depression. When you are going through the struggle, it can be terrible. But the good news is that it's precisely these times when you are learning or growing the most. I believe it's what we learn through our past failures and setbacks that actually lead to our future successes. The old proverb, "Smooth seas don't make good sailors," captures this concept well. When you do have a setback, how quickly you recover and how much you learn is determined in large part by your attitude.

Maybe you are in the middle of a crisis right now, and you are thinking, *It's too late for me to become positive. Everything is going so badly.* The truth is, it can be hard to shift your way of thinking in the middle of a struggle, but this could be the most impactful time for practicing positivity. Sadness, anger, and other powerful emotions are natural reactions, and I'm not suggesting you avoid them. These emotions are needed to cope with difficult situations, to defend ourselves, and to help us change. If you have the strength to incorporate one or more of the principles of positivity from this book into these situations, it will help you move forward.

Maybe you are between setbacks right now, and everything is great. That's awesome, and it is also a great time to start a positivity practice. It's certainly easier to do when things are going well.

Whenever you do decide to begin to practice positivity, you will start building up your attitude fitness, which will help you either get out of your current setback or be more prepared for your next challenge.

I started sharing my story and these positivity principles one year after the accident, and I continue to be amazed and encouraged by audiences' reactions. I'm humbled when I hear their stories and how they expect to benefit from hearing my story. This is what motivated me to put in the time and effort to write this book. My goal is simple: to share my story and what I have learned with as many people as possible. As I've told the story to different audiences from large company settings, conferences, to graduate and undergraduate classes at prestigious universities, religious settings, and as a TED talk, I've realized that this story is relevant to everyone and that each person takes something different away from it depending on his or her situation.

I hope you will find inspiration in the story and value in the Positivity Principles I'm going to share here. In each chapter there are three sections. In the first section, I share part of my story, the next section covers the positivity principle related to that portion of the story, and finally the last section details how to put the principle into practice in your life.

Writing this book and sharing my story is what I believe God is asking me to do. I'm thrilled you are holding it in your hands. Positivity saved my life. It can change yours. To discover how true this is, read on.

1

Amen Run

Positivity Principle #1

It Happened That Way for a Reason

It's a bit of an understatement to say that the first run of the day didn't go as planned. I was unconscious, wrapped around the trunk of the tree, the back of my helmet was crushed, and I was bleeding from the back of my head, nose, ears, and mouth. I had hit the tree head first going 45mph. For real. How does someone survive that? Only because a lot of things had to go right.

With everything that was going so tragically wrong, it may seem strange to ask, *"What went right?"* In a trauma like this, with all the emotion, panic, and pain that goes with it, it can be hard to see anything as *going right* in the moment. We are more likely to focus on what went wrong and ask, *"Why me?"*

As I reflect on the whole experience, hindsight enables me to see that an amazing number of things went right that day. In fact, just about everything that occurred in the accident and during my journey to the hospital in Denver happened just as it needed to for me to survive and be set up for recovery. All of it—even the stuff that seemed like really bad luck—happened the way it did for a reason.

Now, I have to be honest; I didn't necessarily see it that way at first. It took time for me to see all the positives in how the situation unfolded. Since my family and I were so focused on my survival and then recovery, we didn't spend a lot of time thinking about how it all went down. The way we saw it, we couldn't change it; we could only move forward. We did not spend energy questioning why or what if.

That is the main point of this chapter's Positivity Principle: *It Happened that Way for a Reason.* To start the process of healing when you have suffered an injury, a defeat, or a setback, an important and likely the hardest step is coping with the emotions behind the *"Why me?"* mindset and shifting to an action oriented *"What Now?"* mindset. With that mentality you have the framework to start on a positive path forward.

In my case, you might think the only thing that went right was that I didn't die. That actually is where we started. I wasn't dead; I still had a chance, and as you will learn in this book, I am a stubborn, determined person who will fight tenaciously for a goal.

It may sound a little obvious, but if you are reading this, you aren't dead either. It can be really easy to take that for granted. But, no matter what you are going through, the most important thing is that you are still here. You are alive, and you have the opportunity to move forward. As poker players say, you have a chip and a chair. You're still in the game.

Okay, so I was alive. That was a good start, but what else went *right?* There are actually many things that went right. Here are a few of the items that went right leading up to and during that day.

LOWER WEIGHT = LOWER MOMENTUM

In the two months before the trip, I had been on a new year's resolution diet and had dropped twenty-five pounds, and just before we left on the trip, I reached my goal of getting below 200 lbs. I had been on a strict diet since the beginning of the year that eliminated alcohol, cheese, and any carbs at dinner or after. Those things were difficult for me to give up. I did this while working weekly with a personal trainer at a fitness center in Austin. "Strangely disciplined" is how Deanna described my diet that made it possible for me to lose weight so quickly. That turned out to be critically important to my survival and recovery.

I was lighter, in better shape, and healthier. Basic physics will tell you that if I had taken an additional twenty-five pounds of mass into that tree, I would have suffered additional trauma, and I may not have survived. Because I was in better shape and healthier going into this, it also made a difference in my body's ability to endure and recover from such extensive trauma.

KID-FREE TIME

My son, Ryan, and Peter's son, Colin, both seventeen at the time, decided to go on a different trail just before the accident. Wow, what a blessing that was. I am eternally grateful that my son and nephew did not have to witness this tragedy and carry the burden of what must have been an awful vision. Peter, as an adult, had a hard enough time coping with it.

I am also glad the boys weren't there for Peter's sake. If the boys had been with us, Peter's attention would have been divided between getting help for me and looking out for the boys. Instead, he was able to focus on me and efforts to get a rescue team to me quickly. The fact that Peter was able to concentrate only on me enabled him to think and act quickly, which made a significant difference.

DISTRIBUTED TRAUMA

It seems impossible that I could hit a two-foot diameter tree head first at 45 mph and live. Everyone, especially doctors, who have heard this story and know of my injuries have been baffled by my outcome. The only thing I can conclude is that God was looking out for me as I hit the tree. My head hit a large branch first, and that impact to my head reduced some of my momentum, slowing my body as it whipped around the tree where my chest slammed into the trunk. My head took all the impact it could endure without causing permanent brain damage. The trauma to my chest was tremendous, but there was just enough life left in me to sustain me until I got to the hospital in Denver. If my head hadn't hit a branch first, absorbing some of the momentum, my chest would have hit harder, and I likely wouldn't have made it. If my head had hit the tree any harder, at a different angle, or at another spot, my brain may not have recovered completely, or not at all. You might think it was a disaster to have my whole body beaten up so badly, but I believe the distributed trauma is what kept any single injury from being fatal.

PETER'S PRESENCE

I do not believe it is an exaggeration to say that if Peter hadn't been behind me on the run, you wouldn't be reading this. Peter's calm demeanor and quick, decisive action during this crisis made all the difference in my survival. He quickly pulled me off the tree and back out to the run where we could be seen by anyone who might pass by. He applied pressure to my wounds to slow the bleeding and made sure the Ski Patrol was on their way. To Peter's relief, I regained consciousness briefly before the Ski Patrol arrived. Once they were on the scene, he called Deanna to let her know I'd had an accident and to meet us at the Medical Center at the base of the mountain.

I have two short but vivid memories from those next moments.

The first was Peter's reassuring words as I was being loaded onto the ski patrol sled, "It's going to be okay Steve, the Ski Patrol is taking care of you." I distinctly remember how calming those words were to me. It told me that Peter was there and that he would make sure I got the attention I needed. I could simply focus on myself and staying alive. I also remember hearing Peter stomping his feet and fidgeting. I have seen him do this many times, and it always means the same thing. I find it funny now that I remember thinking, *He has to pee.* He confirmed later that this was true.

I don't even want to think about what would have happened if Peter had not been so collected and cool-headed. Peter performed remarkably well, and a part of that was because this was not Peter's first experience in a crisis. Several years earlier he was representing the US and the United States Tennis Association (USTA) in the International Tennis Federation World Championship in Christchurch, New Zealand. He was walking down the street in the middle of town when a large earthquake struck, and he witnessed the crisis unfold in the street around him. It was a terrifying scene, but he learned how to react in dire circumstances during that event, and I firmly believe that it helped prepare him to act quickly during this situation.

If you are wondering . . . yes . . . I later gave him the coveted Brother-in-Law of the Year award.

TIMING IS EVERYTHING

The time of day worked significantly in my favor. Ski patrol checks the mountain as the slopes open to guests. The Ski Patrol team happened to be close at hand and arrived on the scene within a few minutes of my accident, allowing them to make critical decisions that saved my life.

When they arrived and saw the condition of my helmet, they almost called a helicopter to the crash site. But I had regained consciousness and was able to respond to their questions. They told us that in most cases, people with a helmet that looked like mine weren't able to talk to them, so they decided they could take me down the hill on a sled to the Breckenridge Medical Center for further evaluation rather than calling the Flight for Life® helicopter to the slope. We travelled a little over three miles in about twenty minutes in the sled from the crash site to the Medical Center at the base. That may not sound fast, but considering the terrain we covered, it is impressive.

Before ski patrol got me to the Breckenridge Medical Center at the base of the mountain, they had been in communication with the doctor there. After hearing the description of the accident and my condition, the doctor anticipated that after he stabilized me, they would need to send me to Denver. He had activated the Flight for Life® helicopter, and the crew was on the scene at the base when I got there. I was still conscious when I arrived and capable of answering the doctor's questions, but soon after, as the medical team assessed my injuries and began caring for me, I lost consciousness. My blood pressure and blood oxygen levels plummeted. They intubated me (inserted a breathing tube), got a blood transfusion going, inserted a chest tube in the side of my chest, and made preparations to transfer me via helicopter to St. Anthony's hospital in Denver. I was at the base no longer than thirty minutes before I was loaded into an ambulance to go to the helipad.

So, what went right? In addition to the great medical care I received, if I had been flown straight from the mountain to the hospital in Denver instead of being taken to the base, they may not have been able to insert the chest tube and intubation right when I passed out. Without that breathing assistance, I may not have made it.

WAKING UP

I mentioned regaining consciousness on the mountain before ski patrol arrived and how that influenced their course of action. I actually stayed conscious until just after Deanna got to the base medical center and was able to communicate with Peter, the ski patrol, and the doctors at the base. That was significant not only for how the medical team acted, but also for how Peter and Deanna reacted. Hearing me communicate was important for their mindset.

For Peter, talking to me on the mountain relieved his panic. Without that, he said he would not have been able to stay calm and do what he needed to do to save me. Deanna had no idea how bad it was, but as she arrived, she did hear me talk to the doctors and accurately answer questions about allergies and medications. Although I did not get a chance to talk to her directly at the medical center before I passed out again, hearing me speak became critical for her mental state over the next few hours as they made their way to my side at St. Anthony's Hospital in Denver.

FIGHT FOR LIFE

You've surely seen those helicopter crews on TV shows that evacuate patients from dangerous situations and work frantically to keep them alive while they rush them to a hospital. The Flight for Life ® crew did exactly that in my case. They kept me alive during the twenty-three-minute flight and made another critical call ahead that saved my life. The extensive internal injuries to my chest prevented my blood from being oxygenated effectively, and my heart was not pumping blood properly. My O_2 saturation (the amount of oxygen in my blood) plummeted, fluctuating between 50 and 70 instead of a normal reading of 100, and my blood pressure dropped into the 60-80 range (normal being in the 100-120 range) during the flight. Because I was deteriorating rapidly, the flight crew called ahead to the hospital and activated the "Trauma 10" room. That's a state-of-the-art operating room designed to treat patients where every second counts to improve their chances of survival and recovery. Without their expertise and resources, I would have had a much different outcome.

A PUBLIC SERVICE ANNOUNCEMENT

Although it may not be directly related to the positivity message of this book, I can't help but be thankful to have the opportunity to give two pieces of advice to my fellow skiers: 1) *WEAR A HELMET!* and 2) When you rent skis, double check the ski technician's work. Validate that the tension setting number on your bindings matches the tension setting number in their table for your weight and performance level.

When I look at the large hole in the back of my helmet from where it hit the tree, I can't help but think that without it, that's what my skull would have looked like. I would have been dead instantly. If you are one of the few skiers left who isn't wearing a helmet, please wear one. You never know when it will make a difference. I wore one for fifteen years before I needed it during this freak accident.

> **POSITIVITY PRINCIPLE #1:**
> IT HAPPENED THAT WAY
> FOR A REASON

The skiing accident doesn't define me; my recovery is what defines me. I learned and grew as a result, and I have turned the experience into something positive. Finding a path from a setback to recovery was the critical first step.

Even though this situation was terrible, there were many things that went right that kept it from being worse. If this had happened any other way, I might not be here to tell my story. From the timing of each part of the accident and rescue to other really odd but fortunate coincidences, I can see that they factored into my survival, and they really were positives I have learned to appreciate. It all unfolded in the best way possible.

You also may be thinking that this could be chalked up to dumb luck. That's understandable, but when we get right down to it, there isn't a day we have that is guaranteed to us, so whether you call it "not being your time" or "not in God's plan" or "simple luck," the fact that any of us are still here is not to be taken lightly. I choose to look at this as a series of events that came together to give me a new purpose and hopefully help other people find theirs as well.

When we did take the time to look back on the things that went right, we found it really fitting to discover that the name of the slope where I had my crash was "Amen Run." *Amen* is an affirmation of something that happened, was spoken, or was written. I am convinced that the list of things that went right are my "Run of Amens" affirming that what went right happened for a reason. All those things that happened right and all those small decisions by others added up to my survival. All of that set me up so I could leverage my physical fitness, the support I had, the great care I was getting, and God's guidance to recover, and even thrive.

For myself and my family, we still had a long way to go. In fact, we were just getting started on our journey out of this terrible situation.

But, as bad as it was, it could have been much worse. This lesson in positivity was the first of many that we would learn over the next several months. I welcome you on our journey of recovery and the lessons on positivity covered in the pages ahead. I am alive. So are you. That is a blessing you can use to your advantage.

We all experience setbacks or find ourselves in bad situations. They can be awful and have a profound impact on the course of our lives. Counter to what we are thinking when we are in the middle of it, a bad situation can have a positive impact. When you look back on all the setbacks or hardships you have overcome in your life, you realize they actually were opportunities for personal growth. We grow and learn much more when we are overcoming a setback or challenge. Once enough time has passed, you can look back at a challenge and see that overcoming it helped to make you who you are today.

Don't let a setback or challenge define you; grow from it.

It's the reaction to the situation that makes a difference. Although it is natural to dwell on the bad situation and the circumstances or decisions that contributed to it—and it is important to cope with the emotions that accompany it—the only way out is to focus as much of your energy as possible on the path forward.

To move forward effectively, especially when the situation seems hopeless, change your perspective on the situation. Instead of focusing on what went wrong and dwelling on the disappointment or setback, start to create that path forward. Identify the first few steps on that path and take one. Taking that first step is mentally and emotionally challenging, but it will help you shift your mindset from *Why me?* to *What now?*

If you are finding it difficult to do that, here is a strategy I have used successfully several times in both my professional career and personal situations. It is based on a tool I found in the book *Enlightened Leadership* by Ed Oakley and Doug Krug. In that book the authors suggest you ask yourself the following five questions when things are going wrong:

1) *What went right?*
2) *Why did it go right?*
3) *What's your objective?*
4) *Why is that objective important?*
5) *What are you or others going to do to start moving toward the objective? Who will do what by when?*

Answering these five questions will help you create a path forward. Look at the steps you listed for question five and take one or two of those steps. Create separation between you and the situation and start moving yourself toward your goal. You will be amazed at how much better you feel after you have laid out a path and achieved some forward motion. This is a powerful place to start your journey of positivity.

To give you an illustration, I've plugged in my own answers to these questions using this accident as an example of how transformative the exercise can be.

1) What went right?

This is often the hardest question to answer. The harder it is to answer, the more important it is to answer it.

In this situation of my accident, what went right is that I had lost weight and was in good shape physically, had incredible love and support from my family, and had amazingly capable doctors and nurses caring for me through it all.

2) Why did it go right?

Peel the onion of the situation with this question to gain a deeper understanding of what's going right and find things you can leverage to help you move forward.

I was in good physical shape because I am driven and willing to work hard to achieve a goal. I don't shy away from challenges, and I'm disciplined when I need to be. I was able to use this in my recovery to work hard toward my goal, and being in good physical shape at the time of the accident gave me a great place to start.

My family loved me because I loved them. I knew they would be by my side to give me the emotional support I needed to get through this. Finally, the medical teams do this difficult lifesaving work, day-in and day-out, and I could trust them to make the best decisions and provide the care I needed to recover.

3) What's your objective?

Refocus yourself from what happened and the "Why me?" mentality to where you are going and what you want to accomplish by asking, "What Now?"

Stated simply: my objective was to recover fully—to get home, to see my kids again, to re-enter my normal life.

4) Why is that objective important?

Understand why the objective is important to you in order to reinforce and build your motivation to take the necessary, and sometimes difficult, actions to get there.

Why do I want to live? To be there for my family, to

raise my children, to add value to others and to the world—not to mention, life is fun. I have a long list of things I want to do!

5) *What are you or others going to do to start moving toward the objective? Who is going to do what by when?*

If it's just you in the situation, then what are you willing to do? Write down what you are going to do and by when. If you are doing this with a group, get everyone to contribute. Then, whether you are alone or have partners, start moving! Pick one or two actions and take the first few steps.

In my situation, it was straightforward. I simply needed to follow my medical instructions for recovery and do the exercises the doctors and nurses gave me to do. It was simple and straightforward, but certainly not easy. I had to do them regardless of how painful or difficult they were.

I have frequently used these five questions to recover from problems many times at work—often using them to lead teams through difficult changes or situations. It is common to struggle with the first question about what went right. If you are having difficulty with this one, change the question slightly. What are the things that happened to keep it from being worse? What did you learn? What is going well that you can leverage to move forward? Although you may struggle at the time, the situations where you are recovering from a setback are some of the most transformative periods in your life. This is when you are learning the most, you are growing the most, and you are becoming stronger.

Use these encouraging thoughts to help you take your first step out of feeling defeated, discouraged, or disappointed. Allow yourself to see that things do happen the way they do for a reason. Even if you don't believe there is a grand plan or someone guiding everyone to it, you can find something useful in everything that happens. Maybe there is a lesson you can learn about what to do or what not to do. There could be an encounter with someone you otherwise wouldn't have met who will have an impact on your life or you on theirs. It might be as simple as waking you up so you start paying attention to what is happening in your life.

POSITIVITY PRINCIPLE IN PRACTICE

Think of a situation you are in now where you can apply these five questions, and then write in a journal your answers to those questions. I promise you, not only will feel better about the situation; you will also have a path out of it to a better place. Think about a situation you've been dealing with recently and evaluate how it unfolded versus how it could have gone. What can you learn from that?

1) What went right?

_____

_____

_____

_____

_____

_____

_____

2) Why did it go right?

_____

_____

_____

_____

_____

_____

_____

3) What's your objective?

_____

_____

_____

_____

_____

_____

_____

4) Why is that objective important?

_____

_____

_____

_____

_____

_____

_____

5) Who will do what by when? What are you or others going to do to start moving toward the objective?

_____

_____

_____

_____

_____

_____

_____

_____

_____

_____

_____

_____

_____

_____

2

Skier vs. Tree
Positivity Principle #2
Focus on What You Can Control

As the helicopter approached St. Anthony's Hospital in Denver, the crew struggled to keep me alive. The doctors and nurses waiting on the helipad took me straight into their Trauma-10 surgical suite—a specialized trauma room equipped with everything they need to rapidly assess the extent of a patient's injuries and address them. My only signs of life at that moment were a weak heartbeat and barely reactive pupils. The doctors quickly evaluated me for signs of brain function and gave me a Glasgow Coma Score (GCS) of 3, which is the lowest possible score you can get.

With all of this damage they had to triage my injuries, and they determined that the first task was to get my lungs functioning again. They started by putting a suction tube in my chest cavity on both sides to remove blood so my lungs could re-inflate. Next, the breathing tube was connected to an oscillator breathing machine that delivers oxygen to the lungs at a high speed. My body responded, and soon I was oxygenating my blood once again. My oxygen levels had been so low for so long that they weren't sure if there was permanent damage. As my lungs were beginning to function, the doctors started replacing the blood I was losing—the first of nearly twenty-five transfusions I would receive over the next few days.

After I had been air-lifted from Breckenridge, Deanna and Peter sat with the ski patrol who explained that I was being taken to a great hospital in Denver. They said that there was no need to rush to the hospital since I would be in surgery for a while and suggested that Deanna take the time to pack a bag and make arrangements for the next few days. So, while the medical team in Denver worked at a frenzied pace to tackle each of the injuries threatening my life, Deanna tried to sort out what her next steps should be.

After speaking with her sister, Dana, Deanna made the tough decision to let the kids keep skiing with their aunt while she and Peter drove to Denver together. Dana collected all four kids to ski together as a group. She was admittedly nervous, and she did her best to keep the kids away from the tree trails, avoiding ski jumps in the terrain park or skiing too fast—not an easy task with four teenagers.

Deanna and Peter described the drive to Denver as surreal. They avoided speaking about too many details of the accident for fear they would become emotional, start playing "what ifs," and become even more anxious to get to the hospital. The helpless feeling of being so far away from me kept Deanna from asking Peter for any details about how the accident happened or my condition when Peter found me wrapped around the tree. There was nothing she could do from the car, so she just stared out the window at the perfectly blue sky and snowy mountains and prayed.

When they finally arrived at St. Anthony's, parked, and began walking towards the entrance to the emergency room, they could see the bright orange helicopter that transported me on the roof, sitting right above the entrance. Deanna felt sick to her stomach looking at the helicopter and wondered what news she would get once she entered the hospital doors. They hurried into the building, and

Deanna went to the ER reception area. She told the attendant her husband had been life-flighted there a couple of hours earlier and wanted to know how to find me. The attendant asked for my name, checked his computer, made a short phone call, and with an odd look on his face as he hung up, told her four things that nearly crushed her.

The first thing he said was, "He was taken to the Trauma-10 surgery room, which is serious." Deanna knew it was serious as they don't use the helicopters for minor injuries, so this wasn't a surprise to her. She had no idea what Trauma-10 was or what that meant, but it definitely sounded ominous.

The next thing he said was, "Did you see him before he came here?" Now, that may seem like a reasonable thing to ask, but to Deanna it was a strange question suggesting that she may not have a chance to see me again. Deanna told him yes, she had seen me before coming to the hospital. In this moment her anxiety rose, and fear began to set in.

Then, he said, "Have a seat in the emergency room and the chaplain will be down to see you in a few minutes." Deanna and Peter began to wonder as they turned to walk to the chairs in the waiting area, *Why are they sending a chaplain?* The only answer that made sense under the circumstances was that they were too late, and I was already gone.

The last thing the attendant said as they walked off was, "We have a private room if you'd like to wait there." Deanna thought, *No! That's where they send you so everyone else won't hear you scream when they give you the news.* She declined the private room. To her, that meant she was not giving up hope. She felt sure I was somewhere in the hospital still fighting, and so she would fight to not give up hope.

As they went to sit down in the waiting area, Deanna asked Peter, "What does that mean?" in response to the attendant's statements.

At this point, they both began to fall apart, fearing they had, in fact, arrived too late. But, Deanna knows her faith and the power of that faith. She still felt that I wasn't gone and told Peter not to give up hope. Peter, knowing the critical condition he found me in, was having a tough time staying positive. Both crying, Deanna mustered the strength to tell Peter that they both needed to have positive thoughts.

Deanna had a thought in the waiting room that she shared with me a couple weeks later. When she told me, I had to laugh because it's a completely accurate statement and a revealing indicator of my personality. She recalled thinking, *If Steve is dead, he's going to be pissed! He would want to have a chance to fight for his life!* It is true that I would have been pissed if I was dead; if I hadn't had a chance to fight for my life.

I have no recollection of seeing bright lights or anything on the other side; but, if I was there, I can imagine I was upset and pleading my case to send me back and give me a chance to beat this.

The chaplain arrived about ten to fifteen minutes later and introduced herself. Deanna and Peter stared at her, waiting for her to give them the news that I had passed away, but she never did. Deanna and Peter told her they assumed the hospital called the chaplain in to talk to families who just lost a loved one. To Deanna and Peter's relief, she explained that she was not there to bring them that news. Her role was to act as a liaison between families and the hospital. Her job was to help families navigate these difficult, unfamiliar situations. She actually had no information on my condition, but asked if it would be helpful for her to find out. Overflowing with relief, they said, "Yes! that would be great, Thank you!"

The chaplain returned within a couple of minutes and said I was still in surgery. She was not able to get any info on my condition, but just knowing that I wasn't dead was reassuring to Deanna as the chaplain escorted them to the waiting area outside of the surgery room.

Although they didn't get any information about how the surgery was progressing, Deanna found it comforting to be closer to where I was, and her spirits rose as she thought, *In surgery is better than dead.* She wondered why they couldn't have just told her that I was in surgery from the start.

When the trauma surgeon came out an hour or so later, he reported on my status and explained what they had done. Trauma surgeons possess outstanding skills at what they do best—surgery. They generally aren't known for equally well matched soft communication skills. My trauma surgeon seemed to fit the stereotype, and he presented the information to Deanna and Peter matter-of-factly—no warm fuzzy statements of comfort, no "He's going to be just fine." Just facts.

Here is the list of the injuries I had when I arrived along with a body diagram.

Head Injuries:
- Severe "closed head trauma," meaning I had a severe head injury, but hadn't fractured my skull
- Bleeding between the skull and the brain (subarachnoid hemorrhage)
- Bleeding in numerous places within my brain (intraparanchymal hemorrhage)
- Bleeding in the "4th ventricle" in the middle of the brain, (intraventricular hemorrhage)
- Neuron sheering in portions of the brain, where the neurons physically move and sever their connections with other neurons (hemorrhagic shear injury)

- Bleeding into the fluid of the eyeball in my left eye (retinal hemorrhage)
- Bleeding into my left ear
- Damage to the cranial nerve that controls where my eyes point (abducens nerve palsy)
- Scalp lacerations

Chest & Systemic Injuries:
- Collapsed both lungs – blood collecting between the lungs and the chest wall (bilateral hemopneumo-thorax)
- Severe lung trauma
- Bleeding into my heart cavity (mediastinal hematoma)
- Severe blood loss (acute anemia)
- Low blood pressure (hypotension)
- Buildup of CO_2 in the blood (acidosis)

Broken Bones – eleven total:
- Crushed sternum
- Three broken ribs
- Broken humerus near my left shoulder
- Six fractured vertebrae – two in my neck, C6 and C7, and four in my back T3, T4, T10 and T11.

Before he went into the list of injuries with Deanna, the doctor started with a simple statement: "He is as sick as he can be and still be alive, and he will get worse before he gets better."

Deanna thought to her herself as he proceeded to catalog the injuries, *I'll take it! At least he is alive. I know Steve—all he needs is a chance.*

1. Posterior Head Lasceration (Large Clots in Back of Head

2. Retinal Hemorrage (Bleeding in Left Eye)

3. Bleeding in Ears

4. Abducens Nerve Palsy (Nerve Damage)

5. Broken Sternum

6. Bilateral Hemopneumothorax
   (Two Collapsed Lungs)

7. Mediatasinal Hemotoma (Bleeding into
   Heart Cavity

8. Three Broken Ribs

9. Supratentorial Hemorrahgic Shear Injury
   (Neuron Shearing)

10. Subarachnoid Hemorage

11. Intraventricular Hemorage

12. Facet Fracture - Two Broken Vertebrae in Neck

13. Fracture - Two Broken Vertebrae (T3, T4)

14. Fracture - Two Broken Vertebrae (T10, T11)

15. Left Humeral Head Fracture

16. Bi-lateral Polmonary Embolysm
    (Blood Clots in Both Lungs)

SYSTEMIC

17. Acute Anemia (Lost a Lot of Blood)

18. Hypotension (Low Blood Pressure)

19. Acidosis (Build Up of CO_2 in the Blood)

20. Leukocytosis (High White Blood Pressure
    Cell Count Due to Infection)

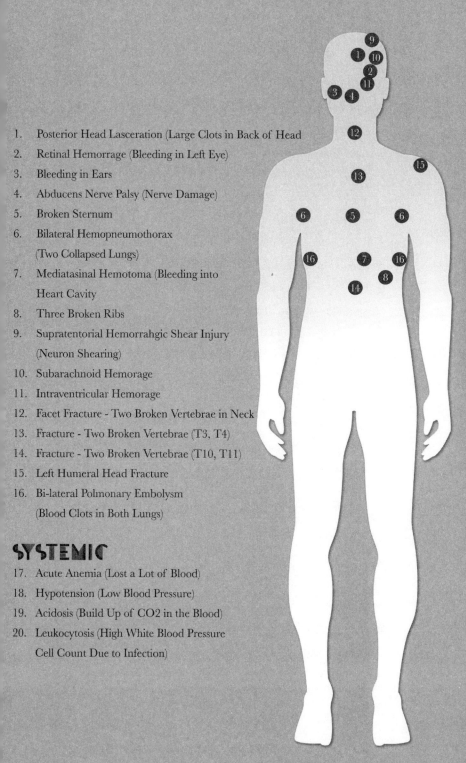

The doctor told her that they had a hard time keeping me oxygenated during the flight and could not tell for sure about my brain function at this point. They did not know if I would wake up, or if there would be permanent damage.

Deanna thought, *Okay, maybe brain, no body, or body, no brain. We'll cross that bridge when we know more. I'm not going to spend my precious energy worrying about these what ifs right now. I'm needed for the strength Steve doesn't have.*

Then he explained that my lungs were like a bruise that gets worse before it gets better. It would be several days before we would know if I had enough lung capacity to survive.

So I was alive, but as sick as it is possible to be, and I was going to get worse. There were so many unknowns. Except death, the doctor's news was as bad as it could get. Amazingly, Deanna's mindset as she sorted through the news was still optimistic: *I'll take it.*

It's All in the Context

I'll take it. That seems like a strange thought when hearing such terrible news. The truth is, Deanna didn't really absorb all the things the surgeon said. The list of problems and injuries was frankly overwhelming and hard to comprehend. All she knew was that I was alive, and I had a chance. She knew my personality and that if I could make it out of surgery and through the night, I would fight to live. She remembers telling the surgeon, "You don't know Steve and how strong he is."

To hear your husband is barely alive and still be able to remain focused on what you do have is a great example of the second positivity principle I want to cover. It also demonstrates how important perspective and context are to your attitude. Your context or perspective is shaped by your history, your expectations, your attitude, and your relationships. Often, as was Deanna's case at this moment, the most important thing to your context is what preceded that moment and your expectations of what's coming next.

Ironically, if Deanna hadn't had the miscommunication with the ER attendant that was so upsetting, the news from the surgeon likely would have crushed her. Instead, it was an improvement on the low point from the hour before in the emergency waiting room. That fifteen minutes waiting for the chaplain established her low point. She and Peter were both completely overwhelmed and frozen. They were in a state of shock, not speaking, just crying, trying to process what they heard, and petrified of what they would hear next. With this news from the surgeon that I wasn't dead, and I did have a chance to fight for my life, she was able to muster the strength to remain hopeful.

God knew I would need them in a positive mindset when they saw me. I believe He orchestrated that interaction with the receptionist to get them ready for the news the doctor delivered and allowed them to start the journey back from that overwhelmed feeling.

After visits from the skillful surgeon who saved me and calmly delivered the facts about my condition and prognosis and the chaplain whose compassion and comforting demeanor helped them process the information, Deanna and Peter were ready to see me. During this first hour in the hospital, Deanna's perspective had already transitioned from overwhelming terror and doubt to resolution and hope. I was out of the doctor's hands, and the situation was in mine and God's. Deanna built up her courage to walk into my room.

When Deanna walked into the room, she was shocked by what she saw. I was in the hospital bed with countless tubes and wires coming out of my head and body. They were connected to so many medical devices that it looked like a wall of machines behind me, each making its own unique noise, flashing numbers and alarms, all trying to compete for the attention of the nurse who was hustling between the machines, the computer, and me. My nurse, Eric, greeted Deanna and Peter warmly, introduced himself, and proceeded to explain my status and what each of the tubes and machines was doing to keep me alive.

It's hard for me to imagine what was going through Deanna's mind when she saw me for the first time. I can envision her tearfully leaning over the bed, giving me a kiss on a spot that didn't have a sensor, tube or wire, and telling me she was there, that she loved me, and to fight hard to recover.

Later, when we had people come to visit who were equally devastated by my appearance and the reports of my many injuries, they would ask Deanna, "How are you handling this?" or "How can you be holding yourself together so well?" Deanna explained that we started at about the worst place possible. Each day, with each little improvement, was a gift. We might have a long road ahead of us, but we were going to have a chance to travel it together, and that was all that really mattered.

In situations like this, when you are feeling overwhelmed by the circumstances and nearly frozen, it can be tough to keep moving forward. Deanna focused on the few things she could control instead of the many things she couldn't. This important lesson is our next positivity principle.

POSITIVITY PRINCIPLE #2
FOCUS ON WHAT YOU CAN CONTROL

It can be easy to fall into a habit of feeling sorry for yourself. It's that *"Why me?"* feeling we talked about in Chapter 1. But life is never going to go perfectly smoothly. We are going to have lots of bumps and bends in the roads we have to navigate. Learning to have the right perspective about what you are experiencing is an important part of living a life of positivity.

Just as there can be more than one way of looking at your own situation, it is equally important to be able to learn how to see things from another person's perspective. There can be more than one way of looking at how someone else speaks or how they behave. Having empathy about why someone else is acting with anger or acting selfishly can have a big impact on your ability to remain positive. That empathy is one of the ways to stay focused on what you can control, such as your response to a situation.

This brings me to an important framework for finding the right perspective, which is an effective way to get past the overwhelming feelings that can skew your view. This principle is something I learned from Craig May, my executive coach at Dell.

The principle is to "Focus on What You Can Control." This means you have to stop and take a step back from what you are facing so you can look at it from a different vantage point. By doing so, you are able to evaluate what is in your control and what is not. The next time you feel overwhelmed, assess your situation and break the elements of what you are facing into three categories:

1) Things you can CONTROL

2) Things you can INFLUENCE

3) Things that are OUT OF YOUR CONTROL

Take a sheet of paper, divide it into three columns, and use these categories as labels for those columns. Write the aspects of the situation you are facing into their respective columns. By breaking up your situation into this framework, you can start to regain control of that overwhelmed-and-stuck feeling.

Once you have categorized them, read through the elements that you can control and determine how you can take a small tangible step on one or two of those items. By taking a small concrete action, you are starting the process of separating yourself from that overwhelming situation. As you make progress on the things you can control, you start to regain your sense of control and your self-confidence. When you begin to feel you aren't completely helpless and gain a bit of confidence you will have more energy and momentum to take another step on other items within your control. Then you can consider putting effort into the items that you can influence.

We can accomplish a lot by working on the things we can control, but we often accomplish much more through influencing. Influence is a synonym for leadership. It is a way to impact things you can't accomplish alone. By influencing or leading others, we maximize our effect on our world.

Although our influence can be powerful, we have to be careful that we are not wasting our energy by trying to influence something we cannot. Before you step into the influence category and pick an area of focus, ask these three questions about the item:

1) Is this any of my business? Is it appropriate for me to try to influence this?
2) Is there a realistic chance of being successful in influencing it?
3) If I am successful, is the expected benefit worth the expected effort?

If the answer is yes to all three of these, you can proceed and start building your influence plan for that item.

Another aspect of being successful with influence is your confidence in your success. To be successful in influencing others, approach it with *supreme* confidence! You won't successfully influence anything if you do it timidly. Influence requires assurance and conviction, so move forward as though you know you will be successful and that your intended goal is worth the effort you and those you are trying to influence put forth.

The last column on the list are the items you can't control. This may feel like torture for those who have control issues, but it is important to understand that placing your focus on these items or putting any energy into them at all is not useful. They are out of your control, and there is nothing you can do to change that. All you should do with these items is be aware of them and adjust your plans to navigate around or overcome the obstacles they create.

Using my situation as an example, I will break down my condition while at the hospital in Denver into the three categories.

1) *What Can I Control?*

Once I regained consciousness, I could control my attitude, my personal recovery goals, and my actions. And that is exactly what I did. I kept my attitude positive and forward-focused. I established my personal goal as nothing short of full recovery. In my mind, it was never a matter of "if"—only "when" I would recover. I focused my mind on maintaining that determinedly positive attitude and did not allow setbacks and frustrations to distract me from what I wanted to accomplish. Even though I was intentional about remaining positive, I still find it a little surprising that I never thought about any what ifs. I suppose even in those weak moments I realized it would have been a waste of time and energy to ask, "Why did this happen to me?" I felt God was with me, guiding me. I would collect all the positive prayers, energy, well wishes, and thoughts people were sending me and use them to strengthen myself and my resolve to heal.

But, it wasn't just a mental game. I also put my energy into doing what I could physically. I did what the doctors and nurses asked me to do. They knew best what I needed to do to recover. I just had to do the hard work they recommended and suffer through the excruciating pain that those tasks caused. My time in the hospital was filled with hard work and misery, but it yielded growth and victory.

In Deanna's case, she had control of her attitude, what she did with the information given to her, and how she communicated with everyone involved. She could give me positive energy and prayers so I could have a positive attitude. She knew it was important to hold it together so she could communicate with the nurses and doctors, understand the situation, and make the best decisions for my care. Deanna somehow had the strength, even with the overwhelming emotions, to learn and understand the medical terms, diagnoses, and treatments so that she could participate meaningfully in critical medical decisions.

While it may have felt that so much was out of our control, one of the most important factors for success—our attitudes— were completely in our control, and we made that count.

2) *What Can I Influence?*

Often, influencing others can have a bigger impact on outcomes than what you can control and do on your own. Influencing others, however, can be challenging.

Controlling my attitude and actions were a good start, but by putting some energy into influencing those around me, I realized I would improve my chances of success. I could influence the people around me by letting them know I was going to recover, that I was up for the challenges that lay ahead, and that I would do everything necessary to get better. I could influence the hospital staff by encouraging them to push me and give me the tasks that would help me no matter how much it would hurt.

Deanna could influence my attitude and keep me positive, and our attitudes ended up feeding off of each other. She could influence the friends and family who would visit me by asking them to have a positive attitude when in my presence, and she made sure I had positive energy around me as I recovered. Staying hopeful, encouraging, and positive, she shared all of the well wishes from our family, friends, and co-workers, and she asked everyone who visited to do the same. She welcomed every bit of support offered but would not let anyone dwell on the tragedy of the situation.

You've probably heard the saying, "You can't control how others act, only how you react." Well, while you can't expect to direct how someone else acts or feels, your own demeanor and attitude can influence theirs, and that can make a huge difference in outcomes. After all, a hopeful, positive attitude does tend to be infectious.

3) What Is Out of My Control?

One of the hardest things we can face in a crisis is accepting that there will be things that are out of our control. But, once we do reconcile ourselves with this fact, we are free to focus on the things that can be controlled or influenced and stop wasting our energy on the things we can't change.

As is clear from the description of the events following the accident and the extent of my injuries, nearly everything else—my body's response, the skill of the medical experts, the decisions regarding my care—was out of my control. I had to rely on Deanna to make the right decisions, the doctors to perform their best, and my body to heal. I couldn't rush it, force it, or wish it to be different.

Deanna couldn't control what was happening in my body. She couldn't control if I lived or died. She was completely powerless over every part of this situation except the medical decisions and her own reactions to the ordeal. She just had to sit back and wait, which is one of the hardest things to do, and hope I would heal. But, by focusing on the small progress I made each day, she kept us both looking forward, keeping our eyes on the prize: full recovery.

And that is the purpose of this exercise—to put things in perspective so you can determine how to focus your energy as you take steps forward in your situation. Enabling you to decide, *What now?*

POSITIVITY IN PRACTICE

Here is a table and a summary of these steps. Use the table below the next time you feel overwhelmed, or the next time you want to think a little more strategically about solving a problem. Assess your situation and break the elements of what you are facing into three categories:

1) Things you can CONTROL
2) Things you can INFLUENCE
3) Things that are OUT OF YOUR CONTROL

In My Control	In My Influence	Out of My Control

Write the aspects of the situation you are facing in their respective columns. By breaking up your situation into this framework, you can start to regain control of that overwhelmed and stuck feeling.

Once you have categorized them, read through the elements in the first column that you control and determine the first small tangible step on one or two of those items. By taking a small concrete action, you are starting the process of separating yourself from that overwhelming situation.

As you make progress on the things you can control, you will start to regain your sense of control and your self-confidence. Then you can consider putting effort into the things on your list that you can influence, and you can move to the next step.

Pick an element that you want to influence and ask three questions for the item

1) Is it any of my business?
2) Do I have the ability to be successful influencing it?
3) If I am successful, is the expected benefit worth the effort?

For the items where you answered yes to all three questions, pick the one you feel most strongly about. Create your plan to influence it and take the first few steps with *supreme* confidence!

For the items out of your control, don't put any energy into them. Just be aware of them and adjust your plans to navigate around these items.

3 Henrietta

Positivity Principle #3

Learn to Laugh in the Midst of Your Pain

Those first few days while I was teetering along the line between life and death were taxing for Deanna. She sat by the broken body of her husband, facing the real possibility that he might not ever recover. The likelihood of living the life we were used to was extremely low. Deanna felt helpless watching the nurse dedicated to my care scurry between me and all the IVs, pumps, and monitors tracking every breath and heartbeat.

Though my chances of survival would increase with each passing day, it was going to be a long road to recovery, and we knew it would involve a lot of time and hard work. Throughout that first night, Deanna watched as my nurse made adjustments on the machines, connecting and disconnecting different IV bags and explaining to her what was happening. Deanna was glad that the nurse had a seemingly unending supply of energy and enthusiasm. With severe damage to my brain, heart, lungs, and backbone, the nurse was doing her best to keep a balance in my body so it could heal and didn't develop any complications that would surely kill me in my precarious state.

My blood pressure was dangerously low, and I continued to lose blood internally. The bleeding in my skull increased my intracranial pressure that put pressure on my brain, decreased blood flow to the brain, and potentially could cause brain damage or death. They needed to keep the blood pressure in my body high enough to survive without increasing the pressure in my head. It required a delicate balance to be sure.

To make matters worse, the oxygen levels in my blood were extremely low, and my lung function was getting worse. To help my lungs heal, the nurse had to keep removing blood from my lungs through my breathing tube to give as much space as possible for the oxygen to enter into my bloodstream. Removing these fluids also reduced the chance of infection such as pneumonia. In addition, the doctors were worried about me developing blood clots in my lungs—a dangerous condition known as a pulmonary embolism. That complication would require treatment with blood thinners, which would be especially dangerous considering my existing internal bleeding. During a visit to my room, one of my original surgeons told Deanna, "He is the sickest person in this hospital." In a hospital with over 70 ICU rooms, that's not a distinction you want to have.

With so much going on, there was nothing Deanna could do but sit and watch and try not to get in the way. My fate was in God's hands, so she prayed for my recovery. She was afraid for my life, desperate for me to soon regain consciousness and give her a sign that I was still there and would come back to her and our children.

One of the things that got her through was being able to embrace moments of levity when they came up. As I relate the ongoing struggle to keep me stabilized, you'll see how important it was that we all found little things to laugh at, fleeting glimpses of normalcy, and brief reprieves from the fear and anxiety.

For example, as I lay there motionless, wires and tubes everywhere and clinging to life, Deanna noticed a wristband they had put on me when I arrived at the hospital. It was a bright yellow band that had "**FALL RISK**" written on it in bold, all caps. It was out of place given my present condition. Deanna pointed it out to Peter and said, "'Fall Risk.' It would have been appropriate for Steve to wear that wristband on the slopes – but he sure isn't much of a fall risk right now!" They both got a brief chuckle from the irony of that wristband.

One day after the accident I awoke late in the afternoon and was alert enough to respond to the nurse's commands and questions. They already had told Deanna that I had a brain injury from the impact with the tree and that my brain had been starved of oxygen during the flight to Denver, so they did their best to temper her expectations about what I would be like on the day I awoke. This was a source of worry for Deanna, so when I regained consciousness the next day, she was anxious to see how I would respond.

I wanted to talk but quickly realized that the tube down my throat made that a non-starter. I simply responded to her questions with a thumbs up. Deanna thought it was fitting that the first signal that my recovery was in motion was Texas A&M's "Gig 'Em" thumbs-up hand signal. We are both die-hard Aggies.

Still determined to communicate and not satisfied with hand motions, I signaled to them that I wanted to write. Deanna and the surprised nurse scrambled to get a clipboard and pen for me. I wrote three questions before going back to sleep.

"Where am I?" I wrote.

Deanna answered, "You are in a hospital in Denver."

"What happened?"

"You were in a skiing accident."

"When can I go home?"

Looking at me with the multitude of tubes and sensors and knowing everything they were doing to keep me alive, Deanna and the nurse laughed at the idea of me wanting to get up and walk out of there. She just patted my hand and said, "Not just yet. The doctors want to keep you here to make sure you are okay." I remember writing "more" to get additional details and explanation of what happened, but I drifted back to sleep before she could answer me.

When my team of doctors heard I had awakened and asked questions like that they were thrilled. Being able to ask logical questions, understand where I was, and have the fine motor skills to write meant my brain damage was far less severe than they had feared. They had been concerned that I would not wake up or would have limited brain function, which is likely for someone who arrives at the hospital with a Glasgow Coma Score of 3. According to BrainInjury.com, 87% of patients who arrive at a hospital with a GCS of 3 either do not survive or remain in a vegetative state.[1] The majority of those who do live do not recover full brain function.

The fact that I was alert and asking reasonable and intelligible questions after arriving with almost no detectable brain functions was remarkable. Deanna had one of her main fears resolved. I had a functioning brain. Now, the question remained: Would I have a body that worked too? Would my lungs and heart recover? Would I have any nerve damage?

For three days, I drifted in and out of consciousness and was only awake for about an hour a day. They performed various assessments each time I woke to try to determine the extent of any neurological deficits. My brain was in much better shape than they had feared, and I did not have any spinal cord injuries. With six broken vertebrae on top of what my brain went through, that was remarkable.

---

1. Igou, Steven (Woody). "Brain Injury - Coma: Some Facts." BrainInjury.com. N.p., 1998. Web. 28 June 2016 http://www.braininjury.com/coma.shtml

Although I didn't have any nerve damage to my spine, I did have nerve damage to what the doctors called the "6th nerve" in my head. It is the nerve connected to the muscles that control where your eyes point, and due to the injury to that nerve, one of my eyes was askew. I also couldn't hear out of my left ear yet, and my left arm was immobile due to a humerus fracture. However, considering the extent of my injuries, I was amazingly functional.

One of the discussions with the doctors I found funny was about my left arm. I was asking about what their plans were with repairing my left arm. Because of the break at the shoulder and the arm just being in a sling, any time I moved, the pain was excruciating. I asked if they planned on resetting it or if they were going to put it into a cast. They told me they were fine with it just how it was and that it would heal well enough. I told Deanna that my impression of what they were thinking was, *It's just an arm. You have two of them anyway, so this one's just a spare.* Given everything else that was wrong with me, this may have been more accurate than I appreciated at the time.

On Monday evening, two days after the accident, Dana, Deanna's sister who was on the trip with us, swapped roles with Peter. Dana stayed at the hospital with Deanna and me, and Peter went back to Breckenridge to ski with the kids. Dana was shocked when she first saw me and broke into tears. I was much worse than she had envisioned. She couldn't believe Deanna was still holding it together. Dana admired her sister's strength, but she knew she was fragile. Deanna barely had slept over the past few days, and you could see the strain on her face. Dana, who is strong as well, committed to being a support for her sister and for me.

Now I have to tell you something about Dana. She is one of those people who could have her own reality TV show. If you follow her around with a camera and capture the crazy things that happen to her, or the situations she gets herself into, you would fill several season's worth of hilarious episodes. Her visit to the hospital included one of those episodes. While coming back to my ICU room after using the restroom, Dana was on her phone texting someone not paying attention to her surroundings. She sat down in the empty chair in the room and looked up at the bed to find that the patient in the bed was in the middle of getting a bath from the nurse and was completely exposed. She was startled and thought *Oh my God! I didn't need to see that!* Then she looked around the room to see strangers sitting in the chairs next to her staring at her. Then she looked up at the patient and realized that it wasn't me. She had walked into the wrong ICU room. Dana gasped, apologized, and quickly excused herself from the room and went back to my room. Deanna saw her walk in, white as a ghost, and asked "What happened?" As Dana recounted the story, Deanna nearly fell out of her chair laughing.

That's Dana. I'm telling you, these things only happen to Dana, and they provide an endless source of entertainment to those of us around her.

After skiing on Tuesday, Peter and the kids packed up in Breckenridge and came to Denver. The kids were both anxious and terrified to see me. Deanna greeted them at the door with hugs and kisses and tried to prepare them before they entered the room. She had been honest with them about my condition and what to expect, but she wanted to be sure to tell them again face-to-face to make sure they understood what they would see and put them in the best frame of mind possible. She told them that as bad as I looked, I had already made tremendous progress, and the doctors were thrilled with how far I had come in such a short time. She reminded them about how strong and determined I was. She told them how happy I would be to see them and that what I needed most from them was their love and encouragement.

As much as Deanna had tried to prepare them, the kids were taken aback by what they saw as they entered the room. Their eyes welled up as they approached the bed and whispered, "Dad?" to see if I was awake. I opened my eyes, and when I saw them I smiled as big as I could smile with a breathing tube in my mouth.

They presented two posters they had made to put in the room. One said, "Get Well Soon, Steve." The other read, "#1 Dad/Uncle." As we visited, the kids brought me up to speed on how the rest of the ski trip had gone and the cool things that happened. We joked with Ryan that since I couldn't raise the clipboard high enough to see what I was writing, my handwriting was now almost as bad as his. Being able to visit me, seeing that I still had a sense of humor, and learning about the progress I had already made, gave them comfort to see I was still "all there." The kids stopped by the next morning to give a tearful goodbye on the way to the airport with Peter. We didn't know how long I would need to stay in Denver, so we weren't sure when we would see them again.

The next day was a big day. The doctors were so thrilled with my progress over the last three days that they felt it was time to address the injury to my backbone so I could start to sit up and move around to continue my recovery. My medical team concurred that the window for surgery was narrow. I was still free from any infections and had grown strong enough at that point to endure a major operation. Deanna listened intently as the team of doctors and nurses stood outside my room, discussed the situation, and came to a decision. It was time for surgery.

Because of the breaks in the T10 and T11 vertebrae, the doctors worried that if I sat up or moved, then the bones could slide at the fracture and cause nerve damage. To prevent that from happening, they had restricted my movement and kept the incline of the bed at no greater than ten degrees. However, in order for my lungs to continue recovering and to avoid developing pneumonia or dangerous blood clots in my legs, it was important for me to be able to sit up and eventually start walking.

After they finished discussing in their doctor speak, they explained to Deanna what was happening. The doctor told her that he would explain it to her in laymen's terms that she could understand, similar to how his car mechanic would explain a car repair to him. They scheduled the surgery for a few hours later, but they still needed her to sign the release.

Deanna had a crucial decision to make, and it weighed on her heavily. She had spent three days watching me cling to life and now, just as I was getting stable, they wanted to upset the applecart. She was not sure that putting me into a four-hour major surgery when I was still extremely weak was the right decision. She wanted to give me a couple more days to get stronger and be a little more out of the woods. Deanna needed some guidance with this life-and-death decision.

We are blessed to have a friend who is a brain surgeon in Dallas who was standing by to hear from her. He could provide the best advice for this situation. She called him, explained my condition, related everything the doctors had told her, provided the settings and readings on all the machines, and described what they wanted to do next. He agreed with their recommendation, and Deanna signed the paperwork.

About an hour later, they rolled me out of the room. Deanna and Dana were there alone in the eerily quiet room that, moments before, had been filled with the noises of all the machines connected to me. Deanna found it funny that she wanted those annoying sounds back. She found it hard to believe, but there was some comfort in that cacophony. It meant I was alive.

When I got out of surgery and came back into my room four hours later, the doctors recounted the surgery with Deanna and explained that everything had gone well. My back was now stable, and it would be safe for me to sit up and start moving. They showed her the x-ray film of the two rods and eight large Frankenstein-looking screws they put into my back fusing T9 through T12. They said each person's bones are different, and sometimes the bones they have to screw into are like drywall that nearly crumbles. They were pleased to find my bones were more like oak. My surviving the surgery was an enormous relief for Deanna, and she was encouraged that I had made it through yet another major milestone. Deanna showed the image to me, and I joked that they must have been out of the bigger screws. To me, they looked more like railroad spikes than medical equipment.

As I was finally coming out of the anesthesia, I looked around my room and saw the posters the kids had brought for me earlier. I didn't remember that my kids had visited and didn't realize how long I had been there. I wrote a note to Deanna on my clipboard about how strange it was that the person who had been in this room before me was also named Steve. I also commented that one of the posters was in Spanish. Of course, it wasn't; I was just hallucinating—the first of many times while under the influence of the sedatives and pain killers.

As the days progressed, Deanna took even more comfort in seeing me attempt to make jokes. When one of the nurses told me that I had pretty eyes, I pretended to flirt with her by batting my eyelashes at her. Deanna knew if I was attempting to flirt that I was definitely recovering. They laughed at my lame attempts at humor, and I loved the sound of their laughter.

About five days after the accident, we received a package from a friend back in Austin. Deanna was sitting in a chair beside my bed, and I couldn't see what she was doing as she opened letters and packages that had come in. Out of nowhere, I heard a long, loud "Hooooonk!" I was not feeling very good at the time, and I could not imagine what she could be doing to make such an obnoxious sound. I tried turning to look toward the sound, but the neck brace prevented my head from moving, so I wrote a giant "?" on my clipboard and held it up for her. As she walked around to the side of my bed and came into view, her amusement made me even more curious. She revealed the source of the strange sound: a three-foot-tall rubber chicken in a purple polka-dot bikini, wearing way too much makeup. Deanna held her up in all her glory as she laughed hysterically while reading the accompanying letter to me:

Meet Henrietta, the good luck chicken.
She has brought us good luck over the years, and now she is yours.
She is here to help you through this ordeal.

I shook my head and stared at Henrietta, not sure what to make of her. I didn't see why I needed a giant honking rubber chicken, but Deanna thought she was great, so I had to make room for our new guest. It wasn't until later that I realized how Henrietta actually did help us through our ordeal. The laughter that Henrietta brought to me, our visitors, and the hospital staff turned out to be some of the best medicine I would receive.

It really is hard to be upset when you have a giant rubber chicken around. I welcome you to try it and see for yourself.

Henrietta became popular among the hospital staff. Anytime someone new would come into the room, she grabbed their attention and became quite a conversation piece. When we introduced Henrietta, no matter who was visiting, they would invariably smile. She set the mood in the room for all of my caregivers. Several staff members wanted their picture taken with her, and by the time we left the hospital, we had pictures with Henrietta and most of the people who cared for me. The nurses late at night would take her for rides through the ICU ward to visit other patients, and she brightened everyone's day.

As friends and family came to visit Henrietta helped to break up the inevitable fear and worry they carried into the room with them. She gave them something else to focus on besides my condition. When they saw that we could smile and joke about Henrietta, that we could still find humor even in this terrible situation, and that there was hope, they relaxed, and the mood brightened. Henrietta was the gift that kept on giving because she offered us, and so many others, the gift of laughter during really difficult days.

I am convinced that this principle of positivity—finding room for a smile or laughter in the middle of a crisis—was essential in my recovery. I am not alone in my belief that laughter is great medicine. The hospital had several positivity practices that also brought some much-needed pleasure or escape from the pain. They had fantastic volunteer musicians who came to the ICU rooms to play music. Listening to them was a great distraction. During the early days of my stay in the hospital, when I was barely alive, a harpist came to my room to play. As she listened to the beautiful music, it occurred to Deanna that this might be troubling to me in my confused state. She texted her mom, saying, *Oh no! I hope Steve doesn't wake up hearing this beautiful harp music and think he's gone to heaven.* She decided it would be a good idea to stand by my bed and hold my hand in case I woke up so I would know that I was still in the hospital with her and hadn't died and gone to heaven.

The hospital also had therapy dogs visit patient rooms. I had several come by, and I loved seeing them. I missed my high-energy Australian Shepherd, and the therapy dogs made me want to get home to see her. Deanna and I envisioned what it would be like if we brought our dog into my hospital room. There would be mayhem as she attempted to climb up on the bed or tear around the room with her ball. Just visualizing it gave us a good laugh.

Laughter is an important part of life for me, so being able to find things to laugh at while recovering was essential for my progress. Like when I apparently asked a visiting friend if they had brought me any pot (since it had recently become legal in Colorado). They laughed at the fact that someone with a breathing tube was asking for pot. They didn't have any, and apparently smoking marijuana in ICU beds was still frowned upon.

As much as I enjoyed the lightheartedness that came from these moments, there were times when it was downright painful. My friends who drove an RV from Austin to Denver to take me home told me about driving through a vicious windstorm in the Panhandle of Texas on their way up. As their first day of travel was coming to a close, just before stopping for the night, a tumbleweed blew out of the darkness right in front of the RV, and they ran over it. It startled both of them. The next morning the wind was even stronger. As they got on the road, there were so many tumbleweeds rolling by that at times it was nearly impossible to see where the road was. They passed cars stopped on the side of the road that were literally covered by them. My friends felt as though they were under attack by tumbleweeds seeking revenge for their fallen comrade. It was like the tumbleweeds had organized and screamed, "There's that RV that killed our buddy! Get 'em!" For whatever reason, I got that vision in my head, and I found it hysterical. As they told the story, I laughed so hard I was crying. I begged them to stop, but it was too late; I had the mental image set, and I couldn't stop laughing. I couldn't get a sentence out for the next fifteen minutes. Every time the visual popped back into my head, I would crack up again and end up crying from both the laughter and the pain it caused. It hurt, but I really needed that good laugh.

There are many other examples of those "you had to be there" moments that helped us take short mental breaks from the serious situation. When I could find a release for the stress through laughter, I found it easier to do the hard work I needed to do and became more capable of pushing through the pain. That's where the laughter really came in handy. It helped to have something that distracted me from my situation. The humor I found in the hospital was part of a broader source of positivity that was essential for my success.

POSITIVITY PRINCIPLE #3:
LEARN TO LAUGH IN THE
MIDST OF YOUR PAIN

The science of positive psychology has proven that a having a positive mindset improves outcomes. Laughter is one of the most powerful activities that puts you into a positive mindset.

There is nothing better for boosting your mood, changing your perspective, and shifting your focus than humor. When you are laughing, you are not thinking about whatever is worrying or hurting you. For just a moment, it will bring relief, and it can feel as though a huge weight has been lifted off of your shoulders.

The Cancer Treatment Centers (CTC) of America encourages laughter therapy for cancer patients. The organization's website points out that "surgeons used humor to distract patients from pain as early as the 13th century."[2] According to the CTC, laughter therapy can bring many health benefits, including the following:

- Boost the immune system and circulatory system
- Enhance oxygen intake
- Stimulate the heart and lungs
- Relax muscles throughout the body
- Trigger the release of endorphins (the body's natural painkillers)
- Ease digestion/soothe stomach aches
- Relieve pain
- Balance blood pressure
- Improve mental functions (i.e., alertness, memory, creativity)
- Improve overall attitude
- Reduce stress/tension
- Promote relaxation
- Improve sleep
- Enhance quality of life
- Strengthen social bonds and relationships
- Produce a general sense of well-being

2. "Laughter Therapy." *Laughter Therapy: Cancer Treatment Centers of America.* N.p., n.d. Web. 28 June 2016 http://www.cancercenter.com/treatments/laughter-therapy/

There are many more studies demonstrating how laughter and finding humor in your situation can completely shift your perspective and have an impact on the outcome of your recovery. Beginning with Dr. William Fry, the professor of psychology at Stanford who initiated the study of humor therapy, and Norman Cousins who wrote about his experience in finding relief from the pain of a rare degenerative disorder through laughter, many scientists have observed and noted the impact laughter has on healing. Dr. Hunter "Patch" Adams built a career on incorporating clowns and play into his therapeutic techniques. His story was made famous in a movie starring Robin Williams.[3] The research on laughter and its relationship with healing has continued over the decades since he began his pioneering work. However, it doesn't take a scientist to know there are benefits. Just think about how much lighter and relaxed you feel after a good laugh. Now, think about what an impact it can have when you are feeling really low or are in a lot of pain.

In my situation I didn't always appreciate the humor in the moment or take notice of it, but in reflecting on my recovery process I can definitely identify those moments and the impact they had on me afterward. It's always good to be able to laugh at yourself and not take yourself so seriously, but humor might be most important in times of crisis because of the stress it releases and the clarity that can come from refocusing your energy. There are many practices you can use to boost your positivity in everyday situations. Whether that comes in the form of talking to someone you love, watching a funny video, going outdoors and enjoying nature, watching a movie, or listening to music, finding levity will help you refocus your energies.

I recently began a practice at work where I started weekly staff

---

3. *Patch Adams.* Dir. Tom Shadyac. Perf. Robin Williams. Universal Studios, 1998. DVD.

meetings with other executives at Dell by taking the first minute or two to get everyone into a positive mindset. We have used a number of different approaches, including watching a funny video clip, listening to a short TED talk, sharing something positive that had happened within the last week in the organization, or having participants compliment someone in the room who did something in the last week to help the organization further its goals.

As you might imagine, starting a meeting talking about positivity when there are problems to solve isn't easy. Many people just want to dive straight into the problems. But, I have found there is a marked difference in the productivity of meetings that start on a positive note. We still talked about the problems we faced, but the tone of the conversation was much more productive, and there was increased collaboration focused on solving the problems. A few months after starting it, I polled the participants, and eleven of the fifteen wanted to continue the practice. Many had even instituted the practice in their own meetings.

Whether it is simply in little, unplanned goofy moments that happen, a comedy you watch on TV, or just being able to cheer for small accomplishments, moments of levity are essential for the positive attitude that will help you through challenges. Regardless of what you are experiencing, being able to find a way to laugh through the pain is one of the best ways to find a path out of the struggle. If you can find ways to laugh and get into a positive frame of mind, you'll be amazed at how it affects the rest of your day.

POSITIVITY IN PRACTICE

Start by purposefully injecting moments of levity or positivity into your day. For instance, begin an event or meeting with something funny or uplifting. Any of the following ideas would work. As you read through them, pick a meeting, event, or simply an ordinary moment in your life where using one of these would be appropriate.

- Watching a funny video
- Watching a TED talk
- Reviewing recent accomplishments
- Complimenting or recognizing someone
- Review a common objective or goal and why it is important
- If you are starting a meeting, reviewing the goal or purpose with everyone present

Try this approach in your own situation. Enjoy any moments of levity and laughter that come your way. To find ways to get more moments of levity, take a few minutes to brainstorm about sources of humor that make you laugh and add them to the list below. Are there people in your life who make you laugh? Are there other sources of humor that you enjoy and can make you laugh? Are there things you do that you know put you into a positive mindset? I've inserted a few suggestions to get you started.

Laughter Triggers:
- A giant rubber chicken in a purple polka dot bikini with too much makeup
- Online videos of people and animals doing funny things
- A few minutes of listening to a comedy radio station
- Comedic TV shows and movies
- A funny article, blog, or book
- A site on social media that makes you laugh

- Pictures that remind you of a funny event in your life or a funny friend
- Asking Siri or Alexa to tell you a joke
- _____
- _____
- _____
- _____
- _____

4 | One Foot in Front of the Other

Positivity Principle #4

Small Steps to a Larger Goal

I find it strange as I look back on it now, but it never even occurred to me that I wouldn't fully recover. Perhaps I was in denial, but failure just was not an option, and that "what if" was not something I felt the need to address. I knew my long term goal: to get back to normal. I expected a lot of hard work, but I never doubted I would get there. In those early days of recovery, I made huge strides each day and noticed the difference in my body. The healing I felt was validated each time the doctors removed one of the tubes or sensors attached to me. Having that visible progress made it easier to continue the hard work and suffer through the pain.

The doctors were amazed at the pace of my recovery. One of the nurses who was in the initial trauma surgery was assigned to me later in the week, and she could not believe how well I was doing. She expressed her amazement to Deanna. During the nurse's shift, one of the trauma surgeons who saved my life happened to stop by my room. The nurse said to him, "Can you believe how good he is doing? It's hard to believe it's the same person who was in Trauma-10 less than a week ago." The doctor, impressed with my progress, agreed. "He tried to die on us; we don't like it when they do that," he said. That comment made an imprint on Deanna and allowed her to appreciate how fortunate we were that I was still alive and recovering so well. That surgeon may have thought I was trying to die, but I can guarantee I was fighting my way back with everything I had.

From the moment I regained consciousness, my goal was to get back to 100%, but I understood that my goal was a long way off and would require a mountain of hard work. I knew the only way to achieve it was to break it down into smaller steps that were easier to visualize and accomplish. I wanted to get home. I wanted to get back to Austin. I wanted to see my kids.

Having clear long term goals, I began to look for intermediate goals I needed to accomplish in order to make the long-term goal a reality. To get to Austin, I needed to get out of the hospital in Denver. Before I could get out of the hospital in Denver I had to get out of ICU and into a regular room. To do that, I had to get off the ventilator, grow stronger, be mobile, and have more of the tubes taken out of me. Now that I had short-term goals I could reach for, I began to focus on daily goals to achieve those milestones. I would talk to the nurses early in the day and ask them, "What's my goal today?"

On the first day after back surgery, my target was simply to sit up on the edge of my bed and move my legs. We recorded a short video of that event, and watching it today still makes me cringe at the way I looked. I'm really glad there wasn't a mirror in my room. Seeing myself would have pierced my false perception that my injuries weren't that bad. I'm glad I was ignorant of the horrible shape I was in.

The next day, my goal was to stand up and take a few steps to a chair by the bed. The day after that, it was to walk to the door. Although each activity was difficult and painful, I continued shooting for and reaching these benchmarks, and the impact was amazing. By Friday, they were able to disconnect the ventilator.

For the first day or so after getting the ventilator removed, I wasn't diligent about doing the exercises the respiratory therapists instructed me to do. My lungs seemed to be recovering nicely on their own, and quite frankly, the breathing exercises hurt—badly. I was supposed to breathe into a handheld device called a spirometer that measures the volume of air you are bringing into your lungs. They had given me a level to hit that was out of my reach, and trying to hit it meant expanding my lungs and rib cage. That meant the deeper the breath I took, the worse it hurt.

It was at this time when I believe God spoke to me. The voice was forceful and not to be ignored. I heard in my head, "Steve, if you want to live and see your kids again, you are going to need your lungs. If you want your lungs, you are going to have to fight for them."

It was a powerful moment. Only then did I realize how important the lung therapy was. After I heard that forceful voice, I became diligent about doing that breathing exercise every hour and each time taking the biggest breaths I could. Each time I did this with such a high level of intensity, my lungs would expand a little, some of the blood in my lungs would loosen, and within a minute, a violent coughing fit would erupt that would bring up the black coagulated blood from the bottom of my lungs. If you've ever had to cough with a bruised rib, you can begin to appreciate the pain associated with a violent coughing fit with a broken sternum, three broken ribs, and six broken vertebrae. It was by far the most painful thing I've ever done, and I made myself do it . . . every hour. Deanna says I did it more frequently than that. The nurses were not worried about the pain or the nasty stuff I was coughing up. They encouraged me to do more, explaining how important it was to expanding my lung capacity and preventing infection and pneumonia, which would be a life-threatening setback.

The nurses and therapists kept me busy and working hard. The worst task by far was the lung therapy, but I also had physical therapy where they got me up and walking. I had occupational therapy where they worked on things such as making sure I could swallow after having the tube in my throat for six days. And speech therapy, which focused more on brain therapy to identify and heal the mental deficits resulting from my brain injury. I had to do logic puzzles, memory tests, Sudoku puzzles, etc. Each therapist worked with me for about thirty minutes and then would leave me with homework to do on my own.

It was a brutal time, but I made noticeable progress each day. The progress made all the hard work and pain worthwhile and actually spurred me on to do more. Soon the catheter came out, and the six-port central IV line in my chest was removed and replaced with a normal IV in my arm. I needed less oxygen to keep my blood oxygen level normal. I was making great strides. By Saturday, one week after the accident, I was moved out of ICU and into a regular room. Four days later on Wednesday afternoon, the staff was making plans to move me from my regular hospital room into the rehab wing where my therapies would become more intense. I wasn't sure how I could work any harder, but I was up for it.

That day, I was able to take a real shower for the first time without assistance. As I took a shower, I thought about how much progress I was making and was looking forward to the new exercises in the rehab wing. It was one more step in my path toward home. We even started discussing going back to Austin.

After the shower, while eating dinner, I started experiencing shortness of breath. The oxygen levels in my blood were dropping even while the nurses started to increase the flow of oxygen in my nasal cannula. I received several breathing treatments to open up my airways, but I continued to worsen. Within a few hours, with the oxygen at its maximum, I was now gasping for breath. I felt as though I was struggling for air more than in any other time in my life. I became terrified, knowing that this wasn't right, and we needed to fix it fast.

The nurses and the doctors were desperate for more information to understand what was going wrong. Earlier in the day they had performed a chest CT scan with contrast, and it had shown that my lungs were healing, and there were no blood clots. Nothing on those images could explain what was happening to me now.

Although worried about repeating the CT with contrast, the doctors decided to do it again to see if something had changed since the images were taken earlier that day. Something did. They found I had developed a bilateral pulmonary embolism—dangerous blood clots had formed in both of my lungs, blocking off the blood flow through my lungs and my body.

They told me the news as they rushed me back to the ICU and explained that I would be on "big daddy" blood thinners to break up the clot and that I needed to be re-intubated to make sure I was getting the oxygen I needed to survive.

I listened to the doctors' diagnosis, what they needed to do to treat it, and I accepted it. I recognized it was completely out of my control. There was nothing I could do about it, but I will admit I was crestfallen. Deanna was terrified and heartbroken too. It was like working your way toward the top of the mountain, having it in reach, and then sliding back down to the bottom. Finding the strength to overcome the disappointment and muster up the motivation to start climbing again can be twice as hard as the first time up the hill. Later in the book, I'll cover the process we used to overcome these feelings. As we regained our positive perspective over the next twenty-four hours, we realized several positive things about this event in our recovery journey.

First, for Deanna, my being in the ICU gave her a much-needed break from being on "high alert." I didn't realize it, but when I was in the regular hospital room, and she was alone with me, she was constantly in caretaker mode, listening to the audible sounds of my breathing and making sure the breaths were regular, and nothing was happening that required a nurse's attention. But when I returned to the ICU with the breathing tube back in and the ventilator keeping my breathing steady at twenty-two times a minute along with the constant care and monitoring from the nurses, she could relax a little. The nurses told Deanna to go to her hotel room and get some rest and, thankfully, she took their advice.

Second, even though we had suffered a setback, I had already made it over some incredible hurdles that we didn't have to encounter again. Several dangerous parts of my recovery were behind me. We recognized that we had already made the journey of recovery to move out of the ICU once, so we knew what it would take to do it again and that we could, in fact, do it.

Third, I was lucky to have survived this complication at all. A bilateral pulmonary embolism is an extremely dangerous condition. I didn't realize until much later that it is a condition that can kill you within hours if not diagnosed and treated quickly. If the pulmonary embolism had happened earlier, before my internal bleeding had stopped, the blood thinners would have exacerbated that situation, and I may not have survived. I was so fortunate that the doctors and nurses responded expertly in time to save my life once again.

Lastly, the hard work we had done to this point wasn't wasted and in contrast, actually saved me. I'm convinced that if I hadn't pushed myself as much as I did on the breathing exercises that expanded my lungs, the doctors wouldn't have had enough time to diagnose and treat me. My attitude enabled me to force myself through the misery of violent coughing every hour. What I endured early on kept me from facing a much more dire situation.

That is why I say with confidence that a positive attitude helped me conquer immense hardship and ultimately saved my life.

"Every adversity, every failure, every heartache carries with it the seed of an equal or greater benefit."

—Napoleon Hill

My goals remained the same—to recover completely, to get back to Austin, and to see my kids. Though I was deeply disappointed by the ground I seemed to have lost, my positive attitude returned the next day. I had accepted the situation I was in and realized the embolism was out of my control, but I also knew I had one thing still in my control – my attitude. I resigned myself to the fact that yes, I had to cover some of the same ground again. I had to get those tubes out of me and get out of the ICU. But, I had the comfort of knowing I had done it once, and I could do it again. So, I got back to work. I asked the nurses, "What now? What's my goal today?"

Just like the moment I woke up in the hospital on that first day when I had the three questions: 1) "Where am I?", 2) "What happened?, and 3) "When can I go home?" I still had the confidence that I would make it out of there and be okay. There was never any question about that.

Throughout any journey or struggle you are going to have times when you have such momentum that you feel no one can hold you back, and other days when it seems there's a constant series of setbacks. My mantra for recovery, if I had thought of it at the time, would have been, "What doesn't kill me, makes me stronger." For instance, while the breathing exercises might have felt as though they would kill me, they actually strengthened me.

If you determine your success based on any one moment, you will miss the bigger picture. The ancient Chinese proverb, "Fall down seven times, get up eight," is another great mantra when you are struggling to overcome a stubborn problem. The point is that no matter what challenge or obstacle you are facing, you can either stay down when you get knocked down, or you can learn something from the last attempt, and then get up and keep trying.

"You may have a fresh start any moment you choose, for this thing that we call 'failure' is not the falling down, but the staying down."

—Mary Pickford

Sometimes it's about looking at what you did wrong and correcting it, and sometimes it's about looking at what you did right and leveraging or repeating that.

I continued diligently with what I could control, pushed through the pain in my physical therapy, and did my memory and logic exercises. On Thursday, two days after it was put in again, the breathing tube was back out. I was able to eat again, and less than a week later, I was back to a regular room and in even better shape than before. The rest of the week was filled with physical and occupational therapy, weaning me off of medications, and removing other tubes and monitors in preparation for going home.

On March 29, 2014, just twenty days after my accident, we left the hospital and started the long trip home.

Flying was out of the question because I couldn't sit up for more than a couple minutes at a time without excruciating pain from my broken sternum. I needed to have a comfortable chair where I could recline. Additionally, there were regulations for flying with an oxygen tank that required advanced authorization—something we didn't have time to secure. While I might have been able to recline in a regular car seat, there were many other complications created by that mode of transportation. Ultimately, the RV was the best (and really an ideal) option. Two great friends drove an RV from Texas to Colorado to get Deanna and me home to Austin. It also presented a great opportunity to exercise my brain as I wanted to figure out how to set up a Wi-Fi hotspot from my phone, connect my computer to it, and connect the computer to a TV and sound system in the RV so we could watch the March Madness College Basketball tournament on the road. I did it. ☺

Once we made it back to Austin I climbed out of the RV and walked with my neck and back brace unassisted into the in-patient rehab hospital and up to the check-in counter to register. They were expecting me and had read all the medical transfer reports about what I had been through. I was not at all what they were expecting. They were blown away by my remarkably good condition, but regardless, they observed their rules and quickly ran for a wheelchair and insisted that I use it to go to my room.

POSITIVITY PRINCIPLE #4
SMALL STEPS TO A LARGER GOAL

The principle of breaking down goals into smaller steps is applicable regardless of what you are facing. Whether you are coming back from a devastating illness or injury, financial problem, divorce, or career setback, you are simply facing a journey of recovery. If you begin with the right attitude, you can accomplish nearly any goal. But one thing is certain: the only way to move forward from the difficulty is to take it one step at a time.

As you establish smaller steps toward your larger goals, your progress may feel slow or even non-existent, but as long as you are putting one foot in front of the other—sometimes literally, as in my case—you will get there. I looked at my goals, starting with the big ones (getting out of the hospital and going home), and began to break them down into smaller increments that could be realistically accomplished each day. I didn't think about how far away I was from a full recovery. I looked at each day's goal, and I strove for that. Once I achieved that goal, I set another. By setting those small targets, I knew what I was striving for each day, and I could focus on one achievable goal at a time.

It is easier said than done, especially when it seems like every time you take a step forward you are pushed backward. And finding a way to have positive feelings about it can be nearly impossible. But, the alternative is that you keep sliding farther and farther away from your goal. The reality is you can't just dig in your heels and stay where you are. If you aren't moving forward, you are essentially moving backward because everything around you is moving on.

As you move forward, take time to recognize the progress you've made. As you pass each benchmark, celebrate that accomplishment. Congratulate yourself for completing what you set out to do that day. Take a moment to notice how it feels to check something off your "list" and hold on to that feeling for tomorrow when you are ready to take the next step. It will help you recall what it took to step from where you were to where you are now so you know you have it in you to keep going.

If you suffer a setback along the way, hit the reset button. Sometimes you may need to adjust your goals. As your journey continues, you will learn new things, and your goals may change, and that's okay. No matter what, keep taking small steps to the bigger goals.

POSITIVITY IN PRACTICE

This isn't always easy, but it's not complicated. Take an honest look at your situation and write down where you are and where you want to be. Be specific with your goals, large and small. This is one of the principles where writing it down and keeping it in front of you is helpful. It helps you keep focused on what you want to achieve and how you intend to get there. I have found that the best goals are often written in the SMART format:

- Specific
- Measureable
- Achievable
- Realistic
- Time Bound

Once you have your goals laid out, start breaking them down into manageable steps. Write down a list of things you can do to get where you want to be. It's like setting step-by-step driving directions:

Start out going west toward Main St.
At the end of the road turn left onto Broadway.
Continue on Broadway for 2.6 miles.
In 300 feet, your destination will be on the right.

You can be this specific with the directions to your larger goals. For example, if you are trying to get out of debt. List all of your debts and expenses. Make a budget that is an accurate picture of where you are spending your money, then look at expenses you can cut to create extra money to put toward debt. Make a specific plan for where you will spend each dollar every day. Write it all down and keep track of your progress. If you have a setback, don't beat yourself up for not being able to stick to the plan; just start where you are and begin working toward that goal again. Readjust to accommodate for any progress you made and any changes in the situation and take another small step. Setbacks are frustrating, but nowhere near as discouraging as giving up.

If it's helpful to you, use the below as a template to help you chart a path to achieve your goals.

"Failures, repeated failures, are finger posts on the road to achievement. One fails forward toward success."

—C. S. Lewis

Small Steps to a Larger Goal

Situation: (Describe where you are today or the problem you want to overcome.)

_____

_____

_____

_____

_____

_____

SMART Goal(s): (Where do you want to be and by when?)

_____

_____

_____

_____

_____

_____

Path Forward: (Identify the smaller steps to the larger goal.)

_____

_____

_____

_____

_____

_____

_____

_____

_____

Today: (What is the one step you can take today?)

_____

_____

_____

_____

_____

5

Ziplines and Light Bulbs

Positivity Principle #5

Know When and Where to Push Yourself

One week. That's how long I stayed at the in-patient rehab hospital when I returned to Austin. It seems short as I look back on it, but it felt like an eternity at the time. I knew I needed a little more care and observation before I could be at home, but I was tantalizingly close to achieving that milestone, and I became obsessed with getting there. I walked up and down the hall every chance I got and visited the "workout room" to do extra exercises in addition to my scheduled rehab. I did extra puzzles and memory tests to stimulate my brain. I even began documenting the hallucinations I had suffered while in the hospital in Denver because I knew the details would fade, and they could make really great stories.

The team at the rehab center struggled to figure out what to do with me because their typical patients were much older and had quite different recovery targets than mine. I had advanced beyond the typical care they offered, but I still needed assistance.

Although I didn't push past my limits during this time in the rehab center, the obsession I had to get back to normal led to several incidents during the following months of recovery at home where I did go over that line. When I finally returned home, I continued my rehab with an outpatient rehab service, Rehab Without Walls, that specialized in active people who are trying to get back to full strength and full lives.

Getting home, sleeping in my own bed, seeing Deanna and the kids in their normal routine, and playing ball with my dog all filled me with a sense of accomplishment and normalcy. I received satisfaction and a sense of achievement not only from the physical changes to my body, but also just by being at home. That provided the reassurance that I was still on a path of recovery and enabled me to continue to believe I was going to recover fully and that everything was going to be okay.

Although these were huge accomplishments, they also indicated the beginning of what felt like a much slower recovery phase than the first month in the hospital. It became a treacherous part of my recovery. The daily progress I saw early in my recovery served as a powerful motivator for pushing me through the painful, exhausting therapy. However, those visible results were not as obvious as my recovery dragged on. I knew that my progress would be less noticeable the closer I came to being fully healed, yet I still began to feel dissatisfied. The change from day to day was imperceptible, but I was seeing improvements from week to week when I would get the results of my weekly assessments from the therapists. I was desperate for progress and decided that if I couldn't see it in my body through expanding my range of motion or pain reduction, then I would get satisfaction by expanding the list of functions I could perform on my own. I was determined to reclaim my life one activity at a time.

Deanna told me during this time that the biggest risk to my recovery was myself. As usual, she was right. I was so tired of feeling broken and restricted that as I regained mobility and energy, it was hard to hold back. I knew I would push the limits of my restrictions. At times, I made some choices that, looking back, were a little suspect . . . okay, some were downright stupid. In this part of the book, my story is more of an example of what *not* to do . . . It's a little embarrassing to publicly write about my mistakes, but hopefully they help make a good point.

This transitional period was really tough because I was feeling better and wanted my normal routine more than anything, but I wasn't strong enough to truly handle it yet. I was tired of focusing on myself and my recovery; I wanted to contribute. It was maddening when I would see something that needed attention around the house— something that normally would be my job—that was just sitting there undone. Those things lingering on my theoretical to-do list seemed to mock me, always reminding me that I wasn't fully healed. All that frustration made it even more evident that Deanna was so right—I was definitely the biggest risk to my own recovery. She feared I would not be able to resist doing the things I'd been told I couldn't do yet.

One of the household chores that especially taunted me was a light bulb in a hallway ceiling that had burned out. I pointed out to Deanna that it needed to be replaced and oddly, that didn't make it onto her list of priorities. I walked by that bulb several times a day for a week, each time noting that it needed to be replaced and that I wasn't allowed to get on a ladder to do it. Because of the injury to my ear, I had balance issues and the possibility of falling off the ladder with six broken vertebrae that were still healing was too great a risk for such an unnecessary task. And all of that, of course, made sense. Yet, there it still was, every day, a burned-out light bulb, taunting me, and I was stuck at the house to see it every day.

Finally, it got to be too much. One day, while the kids were at school, and my wife was out running errands, I found myself alone in the house. I walked past the light bulb, stared at it, and said, "Enough." I pulled the step ladder from the garage, successfully replaced the light bulb, put everything away, and was pleased with myself as I walked past that now brightly shining light bulb. I didn't think Deanna would even notice that the bulb was replaced.

She did.

As soon as she got back from her errand. Oh boy, was I in trouble.

"What would have happened if you had fallen? You knew the risk and did it anyway! And worse, you did it when no one was around! If you had fallen and hurt yourself, you would have been alone for who-knows-how-long!"

Okay, so maybe Deanna had a point. Standing on a ladder in a back and neck brace alone at home to change a silly light bulb was not my best decision. You would think I would learn, but I'm sorry to say it wasn't my only poor choice.

After ten weeks, the back doctor said my vertebrae had healed enough that I could remove my neck and back brace. Oh, what a glorious phone call. He told me I could do anything I wanted *in moderation*. No heavy lifting, nothing that would put too much strain on my back, and *no running*. No running until the six-month mark.

Maybe I could hit tennis balls up against a wall? I spoke to the physical therapist, and she thought that would be great. They said that any exercise and movement would be great for my body and back, as long as I didn't overdo it. If I used good judgment and moderation, I could do more.

So I started with the tennis balls. Because I couldn't drive, I walked the mile from my house to the closest backboard where I hit tennis balls for twenty minutes and walked home. This activity presented an extra challenge because the vision in my left eye was diminished, and my eyes were still not pointing in the same direction. Hitting a moving object with hazy double vision is not easy! But, that turned out to be great exercise for my vision too—trying to keep both eyes on the ball really worked out the nerve that controlled my eye pointing muscles. Over time, I went from having double vision all the time to just having it when I was tired and, finally, not having it at all. Hitting tennis balls was new; it was progress; it was great exercise for my back and my lungs. Feeling confident from this accomplishment, I looked for more.

Maybe I could play golf? My therapists said yes! Sweet! I began by swinging the club in my yard with my therapist. Working with a limited golf swing I was able to hit a few chip shots around the yard and gave my therapist a little golf lesson in the process. Soon she gave me permission to play, suggesting that I walk and carry my bag for the exercise. I did so happily. In May, only two months after the accident, I called a friend and told him I needed a favor: I asked him to play golf with me. He said it was a tough duty, but he would be willing to make the sacrifice. We played nine holes, walking and carrying our bags. It felt so good to play, and I actually was able to play relatively well. Not being able to take a full swing kept my shots in the fairway, which was a new experience for my golf game!

I was really happy with being able to play tennis and golf, and gradually we added activities like stand-up paddle boarding, climbing a rock wall, and workouts at the gym—all of which I got to call therapy! I also started trying to do more of my normal activities around the house to feel useful again.

As the restrictions lifted, and I was able to do much more, there was really only one thing I couldn't do: run. Can you guess what was the only thing I could think about? Running, of course. I have enjoyed running as a means of exercise and stress relief for about twenty years. I was running a few miles several times a week before the ski trip. It was something I missed, and now that they had lifted some of my restrictions, it was all I wanted to do. Once I felt capable, it was hard to refrain from breaking into a jog during my walks. In fact, when I went out for a walk, I would end up jogging a few steps here and there. Just to see how it felt. As time progressed and my lungs healed, I was cheating more and more, and by the beginning of July, a couple months before they said I could, I was running about 50% of the time on my "walks."

That is until Deanna happened to be returning home from the grocery store and saw me running. Oh jeez, in trouble again. She couldn't understand why I would not just listen to what the doctors said. I could do anything but run. Why couldn't I be satisfied with all of the things I could do instead of focusing on the one thing I was told not to do? She didn't want me to get hurt after all the progress I'd made.

"This didn't just happen to you," Deanna reminded me. "You can't put us through this again because you are impatient and do something stupid. Do yourself and me a favor and live within the restrictions you have."

Well, that was hard to hear, but I knew she was right. I needed to learn when to push myself and when to back off. I was lucky to have progressed this far in the recovery, but I also was extraordinarily lucky that I had not hurt myself when I went against the doctors' instructions. I've always been the type to push the limits, so it was hard for me to moderate and stay safely in line. It's just not my personality.

During the summer following my accident, we took a family vacation to Costa Rica. It may not come as a surprise to you, but my new appreciation for life changed my perspective: Life is short. I intended for us to have great family vacations. Since I wasn't working while we were planning the trip, I had time to research what to do and where to go. Costa Rica is a great place with many amazing, adventurous activities. As I looked into all the things to do, I became really excited. I shared with Deanna all the possibilities. The conversation went something like this:

"River Rafting!"

"You've been river rafting. You know how rough that can be, and it's completely out of your control. Do you really think that's a good idea with your back? Nope, you're not doing that."

"Okay, how about surfing? They have some of the best surfing in the world and places that offer lessons for beginners."

"You already talked about that with your doctor. If you fell wrong on too big of a wave, you could reinjure your back. Nope, you're not doing that."

"Four-wheelers through the rainforest?"

"Nope. Try again."

"Rappelling down waterfalls!"

"Really?"

"Zip Lines! Here's one that is ¾ miles long and goes up to 50 Mph!"

"Are you kidding?!!"

I was completely deflated. I wondered, *What was left? The seashell tour?* I wasn't going to get to have any fun. But, it wasn't just about me. I was concerned that because of my situation, the entire family would miss out on tons of great activities.

In the end we had a great vacation. We spent a day at the beach, another day we were guided to see the wildlife in the rainforest, we hiked around an active volcano, relaxed in natural hot springs, hiked to a beautiful waterfall, took a night time tour of the marshes, and saw all the animals that come out at night. It really was a great trip.

Oh, and I did get to go ziplining. I insisted that I was not going to Costa Rica and just do the sea shell tour! It was over Deanna's objections, but I was not going to let my injuries keep my family from having at least one of the really adventurous experiences Costa Rica is known for. Besides, what could go wrong? I figured if the zip line snapped over the jungle, I would die anyway, so having a hurt back wouldn't make a difference. Thankfully, everything went perfectly, and we had a ball.

So, let's take a look back at my escapades. I was on a ladder in a back and neck brace less than two months after the accident. Two months before I was supposed to be doing so, I was running. Five months after nearly dying, I was ziplining through the jungles of Costa Rica on one of the longest and fastest ziplines available.

A clear trend emerged: I'm not good at moderation. I am always pushing the limits.

The lesson here is that there are times to push yourself and times to stay within yourself. I can tell you that this is a lesson I struggled with during my recovery and still struggle with today. Thankfully, Deanna is my voice of reason. I think she may get tired of it, but hey, she made the decision twenty-five years ago to marry me. As much as I don't like it when she does it, she helps me stay within the lines and points out when I'm out-of-bounds. Without her, I probably would have done many more things that would have put my recovery at risk. Knowing that boundary between stretching yourself to grow and improve while staying within your limits is important.

All these lessons prepared me to act responsibly as I approached another major milestone in my recovery—returning to work. My doctors, the rehab therapists, and Deanna were much more conservative about my transition back into work than I was. When they told me in May that their goal for me getting back to work part-time was early

July, I couldn't believe it! I was released from the hospital in Denver twenty days after nearly dying. I only spent a week in the rehab facility in Austin. I was making progress faster than anyone imagined, so I figured I could be back to work within a few weeks after returning home. But they wanted me to wait around for two more months!

They explained that I needed to be patient with my body because it takes a lot of energy to heal, and I had a lot inside me that needed to heal—my brain, lungs, eyes, ears, not to mention the eleven broken bones. If I returned to work too early, it could actually slow my recovery. They used an analogy of a pie to represent the amount of energy you start with each day. Everything you do physically and mentally consumes a piece of it, and there is opportunity cost of using energy. That means if you use your available energy for one task, then it's not available for another. A big portion of my energy was consumed with healing, and it was hard for me to appreciate how much energy that required. That analogy made sense to my logical engineer side, so I accepted the delay in going back to work. As I look back on it now with a full understanding of the extent of my injuries, I am amazed at how quickly that first day of work came.

I've enjoyed my seventeen years at Dell and during my recovery and re-entry I could not have been treated any better. While away from work, my colleagues at Dell not only sent me messages telling me about how much they cared about me and that they missed me in the office, but they also made it clear that my team had my work covered, and my priority was to focus on healing. They assured me they would do what was necessary to keep things moving forward. That was the consistent message I got from my boss at the time and from my team. It was a huge relief.

I attended a company celebration early that summer, and Dell's

Vice-Chairman, my boss's boss, was thrilled to see me at the event. He told me not to worry about my position when I returned. He promised that there would still be work to do after I recovered and assured me there would be a place for me when I returned to full strength. I found that comforting, and it relieved my anxiety about being away from work for such an extended period.

On July 7th, almost four months to the day from the accident, I went back to work part-time for Dell. It was an important milestone because I saw it as a significant indicator of the success in my recovery, but I did have some anxiety over whether I would be able to keep up and perform at the level I was accustomed to. An executive position at Dell is a challenging and demanding role, and it would take a while for me to return to full strength. The doctors said I could only work twelve hours the first week—three days, four hours each day—and then they would increase my hours slowly as I recovered. That felt so limiting, and I knew I wouldn't get much done, but it was a great place to start the work re-entry process. I was ready to go. They said it was important for me to increase gradually because too much stress too quickly could cause another setback.

When the day came, I was literally giddy about going back to the office. I'm not sure I've ever seen someone giddy about going to work, but I am pretty confident that I was the happiest person at Dell that day. I took a selfie as I left the house that morning before heading to the office and sent it to Deanna who happened to be taking a well-deserved break on a girls trip to the beach in Florida. I said "I'm going to work!" She took a picture of her toes in the sand and said, "I've got you beat!" I thought, *Normally I would agree with you, but today going to work beats having my toes in the sand.*

There were two main reasons for my excitement: a sense of

accomplishment from achieving a major milestone and seeing all of my colleagues who had supported me during my recovery. Going back to work was a huge milestone in my recovery. My goal was still to get back to 100%—to get back to normal. Being well enough to go back to work was a big part of that.

Because I didn't want to compromise my recovery or my reentry into this important aspect of my life, I actually listened to the advice of my doctors and didn't push my limits at work. That first week I worked twelve hours, primarily getting caught up with everyone and understanding the current situation. At the end of that week I was thrilled that I was able to handle everything and felt I was ready for more, so I talked with my doctor, and we added another four-hour workday the following week, increasing my time to sixteen hours the next week. We slowly ramped up the hours over the course of the next two months. By the week after Labor Day, 2014, I was working my first forty-hour week, which was technically full-time according to the insurance company (but as you might expect, it isn't a normal week at Dell). Over the next eight weeks I slowly ramped up more and more, adding a few additional hours each week. I had made a ton of progress, but I recognized that I still had limits and was careful to honor them.

Given my history of not respecting my own limits and boundaries, I was proud of myself that I actually listened to my body. I came to understand that resting and sleeping was not laziness but healing. When I needed a break to relax, I took it. When I got tired, I left work. I did not bring work home with me, and I was unapologetic about taking whatever time I needed in the afternoons and evenings to sleep. Rest stood for restoration, and admitting that to myself was one of the best things I did for myself along the way back to normal.

My leaders were patient with me as I eased back into work. They respected my limitations and let me manage my hours and workload. They understood that I only had so much energy and that recovering from my many injuries would take time.

As I was preparing to go back to work, our neurosurgeon friend who helped Deanna with medical advice early in my recovery gave me a piece of valuable advice based on his experience with other brain surgery patients. He told us that many patients were not as blessed as I was with great insurance and disability benefits and often had to go back to work too quickly for financial reasons. He warned that if I went back too early and wasn't able to keep up, it would change the dynamic with my co-workers because they might not understand that I was still healing. When his patients rushed back to work after a brain injury, their co-worker's initial reaction was "He's back!," but it soon shifted to "Oh, he's back, but he's not the same, he's lost something." Once I went back, the assumption would be that I was good to go; but, if I wasn't all there, it would be hard to change their perception of my performance and abilities. It could stunt my working-relationships and reputation as well as my own confidence while I was still recovering.

It was important to me that I not damage my professional brand as I re-entered the workplace. I'm happy to say that because I followed Deanna's, my doctor's, and my therapist's advice and eased in to work slowly I was able to maintain my performance standards. It seems I finally learned how to stay inside my limits. I was glad that I was able to prove to myself that my brain injury hadn't affected my capabilities, and I will always be grateful to have been working for Dell when the accident happened. I know that the environment and leaders at Dell made my transition to work not only possible, but also the best it could be.

POSITIVITY PRINCIPLE #5
KNOW WHEN AND WHERE
TO PUSH YOURSELF

I'm hopeful that the examples I share in this chapter about my mistakes are helpful in making the point that we all have limits and boundaries we need to respect. I obviously had some improvements to make myself in this area, but thankfully, I am getting better.

Pushing yourself and accepting challenges at a reasonable pace will continue your personal growth. However, one of the hardest things to accept is that you have limits, and you may not be able to accomplish everything you want right now. That can be hard to accept, but you are not doing yourself any favors by taking on more than you are equipped to handle at that stage.

As you can see from my experience, it can be tempting to go too far when trying to achieve a long-term goal. Finding the balance between staying safely within your limits and pushing yourself out of your comfort zone in a way that is productive can be difficult to achieve. When you push yourself reasonably beyond where you feel at ease, you learn and grow. You may experience failures, setbacks, or challenges as you do this, but what you learn and gain through the experience can be the best thing for you.

Balance is the key to applying this Positivity Principle in your life. Learning how to accurately assess where you are and what you can handle is vital for your progress. There will be times when you should take baby steps toward your goals, and then there will be times when you need to take a leap of faith and go for what seems out of reach.

If you are about to take that leap, be sure you are starting from a solid foundation. If you are unsteady where you stand now, you may not be ready for a giant leap. Do yourself a favor and take the time necessary to stabilize your foundation so you can safely achieve your aspirations.

If you take that risk to challenge yourself, and you find that you pushed yourself beyond what is healthy, don't beat yourself up. Just use it as a gauge for determining what is too far and what is a reasonable pace.

If you aren't sure about what is too much, seek advice and guidance from experts and people you trust. In my situation, the therapists and doctors knew a lot more about this healing process than I did. Yes, I knew my body better, but at times I wasn't being realistic or reasonable with my decisions. Once I really began listening to my therapists, doctors, and my body, I made better choices and definitely benefited from it.

POSITIVITY IN PRACTICE

In Chapter 4, we broke our large goal into smaller, bite-sized, manageable pieces and then started taking concrete steps toward that goal. In this chapter, we discussed the importance of respecting your boundaries, evaluating risks, and not overextending yourself. There is a balance required—both to push your limits to grow and respect your limits to stay safe.

As you can tell from my examples, respecting my limits is one of my weak points. As I began working toward restoring "normal" in my life, one thing I learned was to listen to the advice of those around me. When you are ready to push your limits, seek the input of people you respect and trust to help you make a plan. If you feel comfortable, involve them in the following exercise:

Skiing conditions were perfect on the day of the accident.
I took this picture about fifteen minutes before
the accident on the way up the mountain.

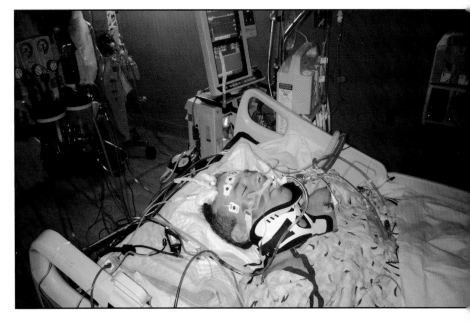

Day One: This is what I looked like when I got out of surgery on March 9, 201

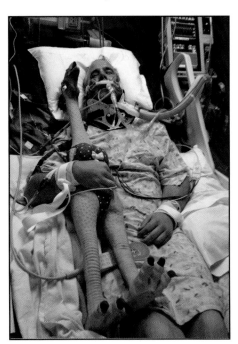

The day Henrietta entered my life. It's hard to be upset when you are holding a giant rubber chicken in a purple polka dot bikini wearing far too much makeup.

I had the best decorated room in the hospital according to the staff. This is one of the two posters that my kids, niece, and nephew made for me.

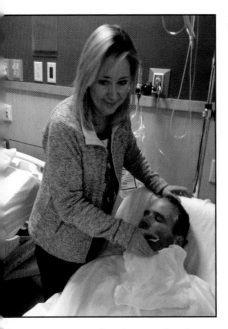

Deanna gave me my first shave on day six, just before I got out of ICU.

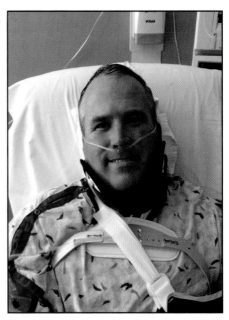

I felt a lot better after I got that first shave. Looked a lot better than a few days earlier

My helmet did its job. This is why you wear a helmet when you ski!

The number of people who cared for me and sent cards still humbles me.

Friends at my son's lacrosse team sent well wishes for my recovery during half time of the game via live-streaming video. If you look closely, you can see Deanna and my reflection on the screen.

My son showing support for his dad with my initials on his helmet. The entire lacrosse team showed their support for me by doing the same.

It was a wonderful moment when Deanna and I arrived at the rehab hospital in Austin and saw Ryan and Katie for the first time in almost three weeks. I looked slightly better than the last time the kids saw me in Denver.

After only five months, we had wonderful vacation in Costa Rica.

Deanna and I sharing a kiss in May, three months after the accident.
My sister, a great photographer, captured these pics

These are a couple great pictures of me with my son, Ryan, and my daughter, Katie.

My first day of skiing again in February 2016, wearing an appropriate sweatshirt.

I DO MY OWN STUNTS

I was just a bit anxious as a took a picture of my skis before my first day of skiing almost two years after the accident.

Henrietta always gets a great reaction from the audience
when I introduce her during my talks about positivity.

1) Look at your goals and steps to achieve it from Chapter 4.

2) Identify any risks or limitations.

3) Ask yourself what you can do to mitigate the risks or overcome the limitations.

4) Determine if the next steps after you mitigate the risks are reasonably within your limits.

5) Get the input of those you trust about your goals and risks.

6) Take action. Take that first step. Create or build on the momentum.

7) Re-assess after each step. Look at what you've accomplished, look at the next steps, look at the risks and limitations, and adjust your plans with the new information.

8) Take another step.

Just remember: You can't drive from one coast to the other in a day. To get there safely, you break it into chunks, and if you need to take extra pit stops or stop a few miles short of your goal, you do that. It isn't about how fast you get there. Your ultimate goal is to get there in one piece and grow through the experience.

6

It's Not Just About Me

Positivity Principle #6

Invest Positivity into Your Network

"This didn't just happen to you," Deanna told me, frustrated after I made the decision to get on a ladder to change a light bulb while still in a back and neck brace. She was right. It was a stupid decision, and if I had gotten hurt again, it would have had a big impact not only on me but on everyone around me. That statement woke me up from a selfish place where I was not really considering how my actions and decisions were affecting others. One of the things I've learned through this whole experience is that we can't fully appreciate how much what we say and do affects other people. We have the power to influence others' actions, behaviors, attitudes, and outcomes. We have the power to create positivity in our network, and we have the power to destroy it.

Although it can be necessary to turn inward and focus on yourself when you are working through a crisis and returning to a state of normalcy, it is also easy to get caught in this state. One practice you can exercise when you are struggling through a rough patch in your life is to step outside yourself. If you can look past your own problems and worries to recognize the needs of others, you have a chance to clear your head and get a fresh perspective on your situation. Sometimes your view of your own problem changes because your perspective changes, or maybe you begin to see that your problem isn't as big as it feels when compared to what others are going through. Sometimes it's simply a matter of connecting with someone else who has been where you are and knows the way out. The bottom line is this: being able to think about something other than your difficulties can be an important step to finding your way out of them.

As I've started to share my story with others, I have been amazed by the reactions. Many people express how much my story meant to them and how much it helped them. What's interesting to me is the variation in which part of the story or which positivity principle reso-nated with each individual. It's helped me understand how important our interactions with others can be. We never know what the person we are interacting with will take away. Sometimes even simple state-ments or actions can have profound impacts that are invisible to us. A well-timed kind word or a careless criticism can make a vast difference to the recipient depending on their situation and mindset. We will never know how much impact we have on others. How I think about it now after the accident is that everyone I interact with each day is a bonus interaction. If I had died, I would have never had that interac-tion. I've been given opportunities to share my story, mentor people, help people with their careers, help solve problems, and provide spir-itual and emotional support. I'm blessed to be here on bonus time to have these interactions.

Before the accident, although I was not doing it consciously, I was investing in my network. I didn't realize it, but by investing in others, I was building up goodwill, and these people were willing to help me later. The personal motto I have embraced for the last seventeen years is: "Everyone who comes in contact with me will be better off as a result." I created this during a *7 Habits of Highly Effective People* class—

an exercise in the 'Begin with the End in Mind' habit. Living true to this motto turned out to be a great way to build a network of people willing to help me. If you choose to live by this principle or something similar, not only will it grow your network, it will also be personally rewarding, adds positivity to your life, and make the world around you a better place.

By living that motto through my everyday actions, without even realizing it, I actually created an incredibly strong network of people willing to help. I had honestly thought I was not good at building a network until my accident. Boy, was I wrong. When I witnessed the outpouring of support from friends and family and finally recognized the scope of my network, I came to the realization that a network is not an organized list of powerful people that you can call upon for favors. It's simply a group of people who care for you and are willing to help you. Looking back with this simple definition, I now realize that I had stumbled upon a great, simple strategy to build a network.

The simple strategy? *Help others, and they will help you.* No matter what your network looks like today, whether it is big or small, this strategy, when implemented purposefully, can help you grow your support system. Throughout my life, just by regularly helping and giving to others, I was unknowingly building my network. I helped others for the personal satisfaction I felt from the act of giving and for the gratitude that I received in return. Building a network involves welcoming someone into your circle and helping them by offering understanding, support, friendship, or providing something they value. I did this to genuinely help them, not expecting something in return—no hidden agenda, not to build my network. I do it not just for the people I think are in a position to help me; I do it for everyone I come in contact with.

As a result, my network really came through for me in this crisis. I credit not just my survival, but the pace and extent of my recovery to the incredible support provided by my family, friends, neighbors, and coworkers.

First and foremost, there is no way I would have made it through this ordeal without Deanna. Without a doubt, I couldn't have survived or recovered without her. She was a rock throughout this crisis. Her ability to keep it together during those terrifying and emotional first few days, her strength and positive attitude, and her tireless support and dedication throughout my recovery made it possible for me to survive and heal. It's hard for me to imagine how difficult this was for her to go through, let alone doing it with such grace. In many ways, she suffered much more than me. Although I had to endure the physical pain, she suffered through the emotional pain and stress. She had to endure the worst fears, navigate an unfamiliar medical environment, make life and death decisions, communicate with anxious family members, suffer from sleep deprivation, and be away from her kids for three weeks. To say that it was a blessing to me to have her as a partner during this crisis might be the understatement of the century. I like to tell her now when she gets angry at me that she only has herself to blame . . . she had the chance to pull the plug and blew it.

This accident and recovery has given me a deeper appreciation for how powerful and meaningful it is to have a supportive partner in life. If you are lucky enough to have a great partner, be sure to prioritize your investment in that relationship above the rest of your network. Deanna is the most important component of my support system.

In addition, I don't think she or I could have made it without all the support from the people who cared for us. I was humbled and amazed by the number of people who reached out and helped. We needed that support to lean on so we could cope with the emotional strain, take care of the important aspects of our daily lives, and focus our attention on my recovery.

Also, Peter not only saved my life by getting me the help I needed quickly, but he was a lifesaver for Deanna as well, supporting her through the terrifying and uncertain times of the first few days after the accident. Deanna was only able to stay in Denver the entire time because Dana and Peter took care of our kids in Austin. Knowing that our kids were in good hands and that we didn't have to worry about them was an enormous weight off our shoulders. Our kids were incredible in how they picked up the slack and made sure that Deanna or I didn't need to worry about them.

In the hospital as well as at home I received a multitude of cards, plants, flowers, several funny gifts and many, many visitors. Each one served as a reminder that an individual or a group cared for me. The effect multiplied because each one reminded me of the other cards or gifts I'd received. One of the nurses said I had the best decorated room in the hospital. Have you ever been in a hospital room full of cards and flowers and wondered if those things are actually noticed? They are. A card, flowers, simple gift, or act of support can go a long way.

Our friends helped us in numerous different ways. Since I couldn't fly, two great friends came to get us in an RV and made the trip home safe and comfortable. Our neighborhood friends cleaned the house, put out Easter decorations, planted spring plants and flowers, mowed the yard, and cooked meals. The message from my colleagues at Dell was to heal, not to worry about work. We received help and advice from friends in the medical industry including our neurosurgeon friend who helped Deanna make medical decisions and our friend who happened to be working as a nurse at the rehab hospital where I was transferred in Austin. This support from family, friends, and colleagues was a treasured gift that enabled us to focus on what was critical and not be consumed by the more trivial tasks of daily life.

In addition to all of the tangible support, it was the spiritual and emotional support I appreciate most. Knowing that so many people were sending their prayers, well wishes, and positive energy our way provided a continuous boost. We felt embraced by it. My work has taken me to many places around the world where I have met people of all faiths—Christian, Jewish, Hindu, Buddhist, Muslim, Sikh, and more. The people who cared for me prayed and sent out positive thoughts in their own way, and that had a huge impact on me. This outpouring of support moved me and was greatly humbling.

I remember lying in the hospital bed in pain and thinking about the people who were sending me their love and support, and then I would visualize their prayers, positive energy, and well wishes surrounding me, then breathe them in and concentrate it into the countless places in my body that needed healing. It was a practice I learned many years before when I did yoga regularly. Not only did this exercise provide a good workout for my lungs, I believe that visualizing and concentrating on healing in my mind also had a real effect on my body. I'm not sure if there is any research to support my belief, but I definitely felt it made a difference.

I sometimes wondered, *Have I made a difference in others' lives? Would I be missed if I were taken away?* Through the outpouring of support from my network I now know that, yes, I have made a difference in others' lives, and that I am genuinely loved. That made me realize just how important it is to continue investing in my network because the difference I make matters to their lives as well as my own. I won't ever be able to thank everyone who helped us get through this time, and if I made a list of names I would certainly miss someone who helped me, so I'm not going to put it in the book. If you happen to be one of the people who prayed for me or Deanna, sent us well wishes and positive energy, or helped us physically or emotionally and you are reading this now, thank you.

Our network did amazing things for us. People showed up for us in countless ways I am only now fully realizing as I look back on it. It can be difficult to identify exactly what you need when people offer help, and it can be embarrassing to actually take them up on it by making specific requests. But it is important to remember that acts of kindness and generosity benefit both the giver and the recipient.

My experience convinced me that investing in your network is vital. By contributing to the well-being of others, you are cultivating and building a network you can call upon in times of need. Not only will you feel good about yourself, which boosts your positivity, you will also make a positive impact on the world around you. By giving to others when they need it, they will be there for you when you face challenges.

POSITIVITY PRINCIPLE #6
INVEST POSITIVITY IN YOUR NETWORK

As I've already indicated, my network saved my life. How can you build your own network to be there for you in times of need? The simple answer is: contribute to it. As in most things in life, you will get out of your network what you put into it. Your network is simply a group of people willing to help you. If you act with positivity and contribute to others, you will see long-term benefits.

Here are a few simple practices to invest positivity into your network:

Prayers, well wishes, and positive energy – No matter what your faith is, praying for someone or sending well wishes or positive energy their way is a powerful way to support them. You can do it privately or let the person know you are doing it. Any way you choose do it is fine.

Smile – ☺ You may not have noticed it, but when you smile at people, they often will smile back. In fact, everyone is preprogrammed to do just that. We all have a part of our brains wired to mirror the expressions on the faces we look at. When someone smiles at you, the mirroring circuits in your brain literally activates the muscles in your face to smile. It's a part of our unconscious process for attuning to and understanding others' expressions.

Try this with the next person you see. Make eye contact with them and smile. The odds are high that they will smile back. Few people can resist. A simple smile to someone who doesn't expect it is a wonderful surprise to them and will increase their positivity. Their reaction to your smile also makes you happier. It really is contagious.

> A smile increases your face value.
> -Fortune Cookie

Once you have started an interaction with someone with a smile, it's easy to move into a meaningful, pleasant, and constructive conversation. People enjoy being around happy people. They will spend more time with them and be more likely to help them in times of need. If you are happy to see someone, let them know it with a simple smile or by telling them so. A smile is a great step toward investing positivity in your network.

Compliment Someone – Another simple way to invest positivity in your network is to give someone a genuine compliment. I would like to take a moment to give you a compliment. You've made a great investment in yourself by reading this book. Congratulations! By taking the time to invest in yourself, you are increasing your capabilities and growing. If you've made it this far, I expect the positivity message is resonating with you. I'm thrilled you are still with me. It means that the time and energy I've spent writing this book are worth it, and that means a lot to me.

Did that feel good? I hope so. You deserve a compliment. When you give someone else a compliment, it increases their positivity, and it can be one of the most powerful actions you can take for boosting your own positivity as well. If you provide the compliment publicly, everyone who witnesses it will get a boost in their positivity.

I learned a version of this lesson in a leadership course early on in my career at Dell and decided to try it outside of work in my role as a tee-ball coach and a youth soccer coach. During our games, I would notice and jot down something each player did well on the field. After the game ended, I would talk to each kid independently and bring up the play and what they did that I thought was so good. Those kids were naturally transparent with their reactions, and you could see each of them perk up and puff up a little. As adults we sometimes don't let on that we need that kind of encouragement and validation, and we try to keep it inside, but there is no one among us who doesn't appreciate a genuine compliment. A heartfelt acknowledgement of our efforts or accomplishments boosts our positivity even if we are too cool to let it show on the outside.

The keys to providing a meaningful compliment include:

- referencing a specific situation or event
- recognizing a specific action or behavior
- coming from genuine appreciation
- being offered without any expectations for reciprocation

Express your Gratitude – You can amplify the power of your compliment by expressing your gratitude and connection to what they did. Share how they made you feel or if it added value to you. By attaching the compliment to your own experience, you not only strengthen that connection in your network, but also you recognize and internalize that positive experience.

Making a practice of recognizing gratitudes can be a powerful boost to your positivity. A recent scientific study proved that keeping a gratitude journal made a measurable difference in the positivity circuits of the brain as measured by an MRI scan. Not only did the MRI reveal differences in the physical structure of the brain right after the gratitude journal practice was completed, but those differences in the brain structure also remained present for an extended period even after the gratitude journaling stopped. This is another example that showed that by practicing gratitudes, through neuroplasticity, you can build your overall positivity and attitude fitness.[4]

---

4. Kini, Prathik, Joel Wong, Sydney Mcinnis, Nicole Gabana, and Joshua W. Brown. "The Effects of Gratitude Expression on Neural Activity." NeuroImage 128 (2016): 1-10.

Give it a try. Write down three things each day that happened in the past twenty-four hours that you are grateful for. These gratitudes could be things you did or said to someone else or things someone else did or said to you. By keeping a journal, you will have the opportunity to relive the positive emotions that come with recalling the memory.

When I read about the gratitude journal and decided to try it, I happened to start on a day that was terrible; nothing seemed to go my way. I'm not sure why I picked that day to start a gratitude journal, but I struggled to come up with three things I was grateful for. The things I wrote that day were really small things. I think one of them might have even been *I enjoyed playing ball with my dog.* But I kept doing it all week. By the end of the week, it was easy to come up with three things because as I was walking around during the day, I would notice things that I was grateful for. *Oh! I can write that down tomorrow! Ahah! There's another one!* It was amazing to me how many things happen during the day that you take for granted, but are really things you would be grateful for if you thought about it. These gratitudes don't have to be big things. Many of mine are simple, daily things like *I had a nice dinner with my family. I was able to help my daughter and her friends with physics homework. I was able to make progress on a project. Someone asked me for career advice and appreciated my input.* Every now and then you get to write down big accomplishments. Those are awesome, but it's mostly the little things that seem to add up and make the biggest difference.

Recognize Someone – who has helped you accomplish a goal. Let people know that you see their value, and do it in a public way so others see it too. I often say recognition is like love. It doesn't get used up when you give it; it multiplies. Not only do you provide the well-deserved recognition, but you also build trust in that person and make them more likely to help you again. And just by announcing the news, you get some of the credit as well.

It may be counter-intuitive, but I have found recognition to be a powerful tool in a competitive workplace where meritocracy is the basis for evaluations and promotions. If you've ever been in a position where someone else is taking credit for your work, you know how frustrating and demotivating that can be. Giving recognition can build goodwill. If you partnered with someone to do something, and you genuinely think they did a good job, give them public recognition. Often, the person you are recognizing will immediately express their gratitude for your role in the accomplishment, and you will get recognition as well. Like investing in your network, you end up getting what you give.

Volunteer – Giving back can be a game-changer. Whether you are contributing to a cause, helping complete strangers, or assisting people close to you, being on the giving side can be a real boost to your positivity. If you are blessed to be in a position to give financially, do it for a cause that you feel a personal connection to. I've found that being purposeful about your financial giving, not just giving to a charity that bought your phone number, will provide you with much more personal satisfaction. If you don't have time to vet out a charity to insure your money is going to a legit establishment, join a giving network that does that work for you. Also, see if you can get some regular updates on the positive impact that your money and charity are making.

What provides a longer lasting personal reward to me than a monetary donation is giving my time, energy, and skills. The reason I think I feel more rewarded by this is because I have a more personal connection to those I aid, and I gain a positive memory. As a busy parent with a challenging career, I can appreciate how hard it can be to find the time to volunteer. However, next to giving my time to my family, my time spent volunteering is the most personally gratifying.

In addition to the benefits that come from contributing to your community and increasing your positivity, you never know who you are going to meet. You may meet a future great friend, someone who may provide a future business or career opportunity, or even a life partner.

This principle of investing positivity into your network gives you three advantages. First, it makes the people around you more positive. Second, you are building new connections in your network and strengthening the existing ones. Finally, the act of investing positivity in others is one of the most powerful things you can do to boost your own positivity.

POSITIVITY IN PRACTICE

Investing positivity into your network sounds simple enough, but it does require effort to make it part of your normal routine. I recommend that you try this for a week and then reflect on what has changed.

On the following pages are worksheets you can use to practice three ways to invest positivity in your network. Fill out this worksheet at the same time each day for seven days. At the end of those seven days, read through what you've written and reflect on it. Do you notice a difference in your positivity or the positivity of the people around you? If you've noticed a difference and want to continue, keep doing it for twenty-one days to create a new habit.

Step 1: Purposefully initiate a smile with three people during the day.
Write down who it was, the situation, and the reaction:

Day	Who	Where/When	Reaction
1			
2			
3			
4			
5			
6			
7			

Step 2: Go out of your way to provide a genuine complement to three different people:

Day	Who	Compliment	Reaction
1			
2			
3			
4			
5			
6			
7			

Step 3: Write down three things you are grateful for. This can be something you did or said or something someone did or said to you.

Day 1
Day 2
Day 3
Day 4
Day 5
Day 6
Day 7

7 Get Your Head Right First

Positivity Principle #7

Creating a Positivity Practice

As I've said earlier, we all have setbacks and challenges. They are a part of life. It's how we deal with them that is in our control. The skiing accident was a big setback for my life, and my attitude was positive as I went through my recovery. It was the disappointments and setbacks during my recovery where I had to work hard to stay positive. One of the most pronounced emotional struggles for me was when I suffered the pulmonary embolism. My recovery was progressing remarkably well, but on day nine, I took a big step backwards. I went from a regular hospital room back to the ICU. I went from breathing on my own to having a breathing tube inserted again.

Although I should have felt happy I was alive, I was terribly disappointed, angry, frustrated, and sad. It meant that I was farther away from my goal of going home. Both Deanna and I were emotional and it was one of the few times in Denver when we didn't have a visitor in town to help with the emotional support. Deanna was all alone with this, and it was the only time in the hospital that I saw her cry.

But we had no choice but to come to terms with the situation, and cope with the feelings so that we could move on. I had my pity party, sat with the feelings, and felt sorry for myself for a little while. Once I gave myself the time to come to terms with the situation, the emotions subsided, and I realized I still had the same goals. I still had the same mountain to climb. I had already cleared part of the path, and I knew what it would take to regain that ground.

It took less than a day for me to go through this mental process, which seems fast to me as I look back on it. It's hard for me to explain how I was able to work through the emotions that quickly. Every situation is different, and everyone will sort through their emotions differently, but the key thing to resist is getting stuck in the *Why me?* mentality. Not everyone will be able to sort through the complexities of feeling defeated and discouraged that quickly. If it takes you a while, that's okay. Don't beat yourself up as you go through the process just don't get stuck. Move as quickly as you can from *"Why me?"* to *"What now?"*

The other disappointment and frustration I experienced came a couple weeks later when we were starting to make plans to return to Austin. Our friends had picked up the RV and were already on the road to Denver to get us when I started running a fever. The hospital postponed my release indefinitely. They needed to determine what part of my body was infected and the strain of bacteria that was causing the infection. They said I couldn't go home until they knew what was going on and had an effective treatment in place. Ugh.

I was so close to getting out—only a day or two away from that huge milestone of being released from the hospital and returning to Austin to see my kids. Now my forward momentum was impeded again, and worse than that, it was for an indefinite amount of time. It was extremely frustrating, but the doctor's decision made sense. I was angry, but there wasn't really anyone to be angry at. There was nothing I could have done to prevent the infection, and being upset certainly wasn't going to help it go away. The doctors soon determined that I had developed a bladder infection with common bacteria that was easily treatable with antibiotics, but they still wouldn't let me go until they saw me improve.

I decided the best use of the extra couple of days in the hospital was to focus on getting stronger and do my therapies and exercises. During that time, I was able to be weaned completely off of oxygen and increase my stamina and strength to walk farther around the halls of the hospital. Getting off of oxygen made the trip home much easier and put me in much better condition for the travel. My doctors gave us strict instructions for mandatory rest stops every two hours where I was to get out and walk around in order to prevent blood clots from forming in my legs. This increase in exercise actually made me stronger. Although I was afraid the ride home would wear me out and cause another setback, the additional time in the hospital benefitted me because I was much stronger and had the stamina to endure the long trip.

You may be thinking that regaining the right perspective when things go awry sounds good, but screaming at me, "Okay, but how do I do that, Steve?!" There are a number of potential paths to this way of thinking, but one of the most effective I've found has been starting a morning ritual and a mindfulness practice. In the "Positivity in Practice" section of this chapter, I describe what that means and how you can use it as well. But before we get to that, the first step is, as the title states, to get your head right first. To do that you have to understand what it means to confront disappointment—to put it in its proper place—and then determine what moves are the right ones to get you moving forward.

Dealing with Disappointment

So, how exactly do you deal with negative feelings when they come up? How do you deal with anger and frustration without allowing it to get you off track? First, acknowledge those feelings because trying to pretend they aren't there is as destructive as letting them get out of control. Intense feelings are your mind's way of telling you that something important is happening to you.

Next, take some time to isolate what the emotion is trying to tell you. Something is happening that is important to you. Sometimes we need to simply sit with the emotion, understand what is driving it, and then work through it. The only way to work through this feeling is to face it. Pushing it aside or ignoring it is just delaying the inevitable. Whatever is at the root is going to keep pushing you to confront it head on. Understanding and accepting the event or situation that is causing the intense emotion is the only way to resolve it. Once you do this, you may start to uncover choices or actions you can make to move forward more successfully.

As my recovery stretched from weeks into months, and the progress slowed, I started to feel frustrated and worn out. In the early stages of rehab, I was progressing by leaps and bounds. All of my hard work was yielding visible results, and I could mark my improvement each day. That was incredibly motivating and kept me going even when the work was painful and exhausting. As time went on, I still saw week over week and month over month improvements, but I no longer was getting the daily payoffs. That made it mentally much harder to stick with the necessary rehab work. I had occupational, physical, and speech therapists who each came by my house once a week to work with me, evaluate my progress, and give me new exercises for homework. Though it was helpful to get their assessments and affirmations of how far I had come from the previous week, without the daily changes, my enthusiasm and drive tended to wane in the days that would follow their visit.

To stay tapped in to my motivation to push through, I had to keep reminding myself of my goal: to recover completely. Even though the pace was slower, I was still moving forward. I had to remember that I had already closed the gap between death and recovery so much that the amount of ground I had to cover was going to diminish more with each week. Feeling you are stalled, especially after experiencing great momentum, can be incredibly frustrating. Having a positive mindset can help you to see beyond the moment in these circumstances and see the bigger picture.

Making the Right Moves

In addition to the struggle that comes from feeling stuck, it is also common to feel the urgency to just be doing something. One of the hardest things for me to do was (and still is) to be still and rest. I wanted to be up and going and doing something. I felt guilty about taking naps because it seemed like wasted time—time when I could be getting stronger and getting caught up on work. It took a while, but my perspective has changed. I finally came to understand that sleeping was vitally important to my healing and that during this downtime I was actually getting stronger. It was a big relief to let go of the guilt I felt when I took naps, and it's great to have this whole new perspective on naps. Maybe I'll go take one now. ☺

Many people think of positivity as just having an optimistic outlook and a sunny disposition. But let's be honest, how hard is it to be positive and happy when things are good? We have an automatic and unavoidably hopeful perspective when all is right with the world. The challenge is to remain positive and keep moving forward when things aren't going your way. But that's exactly when the principle of positivity has the greatest potential to make a difference in your life.

Think of all the setbacks you've already overcome in your life. When you were going through them, it may have been miserable, but when you look back at it now, you will probably find that they changed you. Likely, you will find that those are the times when you grew the most. Overcoming those challenges made you who you are today. Through your suffering you learned, you grew, you became stronger. You and I will have setbacks in the future. We don't want them, and we won't like it when we have them, but like our past challenges, these too will provide new opportunities to learn and grow.

Experiencing a setback or a challenge may be the hardest time to find the courage to move forward or find encouragement, but that can be a perfect time to start a regimen for positivity. It could mean simply pausing in the midst of your disappointment to see what benefit there could be in the setback. Ask yourself, *How can I make this work to my advantage? What is useful for me in this situation? What can I learn?* But, I'll warn you, having done it myself in a difficult place, it also happens to be one of the hardest times to start it.

POSITIVITY PRINCIPLE #7
CREATING A POSITIVITY PRACTICE

A lot of what I've learned about positivity came after my recovery when I started speaking about my accident and the journey back to health. I read several books on the subject—some from psychologists with experience in the field of positive psychology, some by doctors who emphasize the impact of your diet on your brain and your positivity, and some just by people with experiences like mine.

All of this was fascinating to me. I had discovered the effectiveness of this approach in my own life without knowing much about it, and I wanted to learn more.

In my research on positivity, I learned about the miracle of neuroplasticity—the fact that your brain is constantly physically changing—with everything you learn or practice intentionally. This concept also works for increasing positivity! I will dig deeper into this concept in the next chapter, but it's important to introduce now because it is the reason why a regular positivity practice can be so impactful. You may consider yourself an optimist or a pessimist today, but all you have to do to improve your positivity is put focused effort into practicing it. Each time you do something to boost your positivity, you will strengthen those circuits in your brain.

One of the books I found especially impactful was *The Miracle Morning* by Hal Elrod. His story details his recovery from a car accident that nearly killed him. I was particularly interested in what he did to overcome the depression that came with his struggle to recover. He adopted a morning ritual that he called the "Miracle Morning."[5]

It was about a year after returning to work when I came across his book and began implementing a version of this ritual in my own life. I followed the practice for over 100 days (not consecutively) hoping to increase my positivity and overcome new challenges in my life. It was a significant time investment to be sure, but it really did make a difference in my attitude. In fact, as I'm recalling that experience, I feel the urge to do another round of my positivity practice.

The positivity practice is a process that, as I view it, is all about shaping your mindset so it frames how you approach the rest of your day. In my practice, I started with a short five-minute meditation to

---

5. Elrod, Hal. *The Miracle Morning.* US: Hal Elrod, 2012.

calm my mind. (Well, I attempted to. My dog saw my sitting still on the floor as an invitation for play.) Meditation comes in many forms and you can approach it in whatever way works for you. There are extensive tools as well for guiding you in meditation and there is no rule about which style you should try. The important thing is just to give your mind time for stillness at the beginning of each day to start off with your mind in a calm, clear, positive state.

The next step involved setting my intentions. I recited a list of things I intended for my life. I probably have too many—I have fifteen on my list—but I can't think of any I would cut. I share them with you below so you can have a sense of what I mean by intentions, but yours don't have to model mine at all, and you certainly don't have to have as many as I do. In fact, it's probably better to start with just a couple.

My Intentions:

- I will enjoy this moment.
- I will enjoy this day.
- Everyone who comes in contact with me today will be better off as a result.
- I will be a great husband, father, and friend.
- I will make the people around me more positive.
- I will make the world more positive.
- I will help companies achieve better results by helping their leaders lead with positivity and get better individual outcomes from everyone in the company
- I will write a book. (This one!)
- I will give a TED talk. (Done! TEDxTAMU 4/16/16)
- I will be an inspirational speaker.
- I will make Dell be more profitable.

- I will be financially independent.
- I will own a mountain house.
- I will walk the John Muir trail.
- I will see Haley's comet with family, and I will do it with a clear mind. (I will be ninety-four-years-old when it comes back!)

The next step is to do twenty minutes of exercise. Maybe that's a quick jog, some calisthenics and core work, or some yoga. Obviously, you can follow whatever exercise regimen you already have in place, but the idea is to make sure you get in at least twenty minutes of some kind of physical activity. I don't have to tell you how beneficial exercise is to your physical, mental, and spiritual health. But, starting the day with a manageable amount of exercise is a great way to begin your positivity practice.

The last part of my positivity practice was to journal. There are two things I included each day: 1) I listed what I would do that day to move toward one or more of my intentions, and 2) I would journal my "gratitudes"—what I was grateful for that had happened in the last twenty-four hours. My journal might be just a couple of sentences, or it could be a couple of pages. The purpose of the journal was, first, to help myself become focused and deliberate about how I approached the day, and, second, to be mindful of what was happening around me that contributed to the progress I had made toward those intentions. By doing these two things I stopped letting life happen to me and started really embracing and enjoying the life I'd been given a second chance to live.

The entire routine took about an hour each morning, and I found it made a significant difference in how I felt for the entire day. I had more energy, better mental clarity, and really felt the progress I was making toward my intentions. On the mornings I was rushed, I still did something, just something shorter, and sometimes recited my intentions while I was doing other morning activities.

As happens with all of us, life gets in the way, and we let things that are beneficial fall by the wayside. Isn't it funny how we often let the stuff that is good for us lapse, and we keep the bad habits going? I could easily beat myself up over dropping this practice, especially since I'm writing about it in my book and telling you to do it! But, that is not part of a positive attitude, and it is the perfect illustration for the positivity practice of this chapter. You aren't always going to feel positive. You aren't always going to do the things you know are best for you and most helpful for your state of mind. That in no way means you are a failure in positivity. The only way that would be true is if you never tried again.

So, just as you may be facing a day or a year when you feel nothing is going right, and you need help finding the encouragement to keep trying, I have faced those challenges too, and writing this book has motivated me to get back into a positivity ritual every morning.

POSITIVITY IN PRACTICE

A positivity practice is one you can incorporate into every day, and it will be a key part of helping you refocus when you are not feeling positive. You won't find a better way to shake off negativity than to begin expressing gratitude. There is nothing better for reenergizing yourself than to spend time thinking about how you want to impact your day and setting a plan for accomplishing it.

Start tomorrow on your own morning routine that centers you mentally, physically, and spiritually. For more info on it, and for some tips on how to do the really hard part of this routine —actually getting up when the alarm goes off in the morning—get Hal's book, *The Miracle Morning*. Here is the outline of what I did:

Meditate – five minutes

Recite Intentions – five minutes

Exercise – twenty minutes

Read something intellectually stimulating – fifteen minutes

Journal three gratitude's and intentions for the day – fifteen minutes

8 Post-Traumatic Growth

Positivity Principle #8

Embrace Growing Pains and Learn from Your Struggles

One of the challenges I had in the hospital in Denver that I had to overcome was a four-day episode of psychosis where I was hallucinating. It happened around the time I had the breathing tube removed, a few days before the pulmonary embolism. The hallucinations started out benign—humorous even—and I knew they weren't real. The first time I experienced psychosis was when I closed my eyes to go to sleep, and instead of my vision going dark, I was in a large convention hall filled with people and booths featuring remote control racing cars, gadgets, and other technologies that could give racers an edge. It was as real as it could be . . . and bizarre. As an engineer, I enjoyed seeing a bunch of robotics and electronics that don't really exist. (Now I wish I'd remembered some of it. I might have a gold mine sitting in my imagination.) When I got tired of the convention and the races, I would open my eyes and be back in my room. When I closed my eyes, I was back at the races. While these hallucinations weren't scary, they were exhausting because I was unable to rest as long as my mind kept taking me on a trip each time I tried to sleep.

To make matters worse, over the coming days the hallucinations went from friendly to sinister. Eventually my visions became images of my wife and children being blackmailed and attacked with threats for the attacks to escalate if they didn't follow instructions. On the wall in my hospital room I hallucinated the equivalent of a Twitter feed that was streaming descriptions of events that were really happening and threats related to those events. They included things such as, *I see your wife going back to her hotel room; I think I'll pay her a visit.* It was an awful experience that lasted for days. Being helpless to do anything about it made me incredibly anxious. In another hallucination, I listened to a plot by hackers who had hacked into the hospital network and were trying to kill me by controlling the doses of painkillers and other drugs coming into my body through the IV machines attached to the hospital network. It was terrifying, and I started having a hard time knowing what was real and what wasn't. I was afraid to talk to my wife or the hospital staff about it because I thought they wouldn't believe me, and they would worry about my brain injury.

Needless to say, this situation made staying positive extremely difficult. Not only was I in great physical pain, fighting for my lungs with the breathing exercises, I was desperate for sleep. That was by far the most mentally challenging time of my recovery. But, somehow my positive attitude was strong enough to overcome those challenges. I was thankful when the hallucinations stopped after four days because they were definitely a drain on my energy and my ability to stay positive. I've learned later that those types of hallucinations are common and are part of a condition called ICU psychosis. I'm not sure if it was my brain injury, the drugs I was on, or the combination of the two, but from that experience I have a much deeper appreciation for people who suffer from hallucinations.

About two months into my recovery the psychologist who was evaluating me for the brain injury asked, "Is there anything that happened in your life you would like to change?" My answer was, "Yes, I wouldn't have skied into that tree!"

If you were to ask me that question now, I would tell you that I wouldn't change anything - even running into that tree. As I said in Chapter 1, I believe everything happens for a reason. As I reflect on it now, approaching the two-year anniversary of the accident, I grew as a result of the experience, and it has made me stronger. Now that I am on the other side of my recovery, and I'm starting to share the lessons I've learned, I see how much my story is helping other people. They are finding inspiration in my experience, and they are changing their attitudes and lives as a result of hearing what I went through, the lessons I learned from it, and how I have applied positivity principles to my life. The experience I have when sharing my story and inspiring others is extremely powerful to me, and it wouldn't be happening if I hadn't run into that tree and recovered as I did.

Now, don't get me wrong. I had plenty of days during my recovery when I wished the accident had never happened. It took time for me to see anything good coming out of it. It took quite a while for me to get to this mindset. It's natural when you are in the midst of recovering from a setback to overlook the potential positives that can come out of it. That wisdom only comes with the passage of time.

As I recovered and was pushing through my therapies, I listened to numerous TED talks and other sources of encouragement and learning. For obvious reasons I was especially interested in the brain and healing, and about six months into my recovery, I came across a TED talk given by Jane McGonigal, a game designer who suffered severe setbacks after a concussion. Her talk was titled, "The Game that Can Give You Ten Extra Years of Life." In the talk she discusses a concept scientists call "Post Traumatic Growth" (PTG), which is essentially the opposite of Post-Traumatic Stress Disorder (PTSD). PTG happens when someone reacts to a stressful event in a positive way, becoming stronger and happier. In the talk, she shared the five most common things people say are different about them as a result of PTG:

- My priorities have changed, and I'm not afraid to do what makes me happy.
- I feel closer to my friends and family.
- I understand myself better; I know who I really am now.
- I have a new sense of meaning and purpose.
- I am better able to focus on my goals and dreams.

I was dumbfounded when I heard it because I could relate to each of those statements. When she completed the list I turned to my wife and said, "That's me!" What I was experiencing was actually recognized in science. It had a name, and there were others like me! It was comforting to know that I was part of a group and that I wasn't alone or delusional.

Later in the talk, she described four categories of resilience that she built into the game she created called "Superbetter." She used this game to heal from her concussion, and it has worked for her and many others. The positivity principles in this book fall into the four categories of resilience she described:

- Mental Resilience – Willpower gives you the ability to get your head right first so you will have the strength to overcome mental obstacles.
- Emotional Resilience – Positive emotions such as love, happiness, and satisfaction improve your health and your ability to

overcome obstacles.

- Social Resilience – Showing gratitude to others for what they do for you, making someone smile by smiling at them, or giving a genuine compliment to one person each day all boost your ability to accomplish your goals.
- Physical Resilience – Moving, standing, sitting in a positive posture, and exercising all help you increase your physical resilience and enable your body to heal better.[6]

All of this made complete sense to me, but what I couldn't quite understand is why I experienced PTG instead of PTSD. I'm thankful I did, but I was curious about why I had this experience rather than the opposite. I'm not sure I would have survived at all if I had experienced PTSD instead, and I'm sure I wouldn't have recovered as well had I not enjoyed the willpower and motivation to do all the hard work necessary to recover. What I suspect is that I was wired this way when the accident happened. The important question is—have I always been this way, or did I develop into this? As I reflect on this question, I realize that I had been building up my mental, emotional, social, and physical resilience throughout my life without consciously thinking about it, and when I needed that resilience most, it was there for me.

For example, I can point to practices and behaviors I had in place before my injury that contributed to my mental resiliency. Throughout my life I have eagerly accepted challenges and taken on complex jobs. From leadership roles I had in college, to the corporate culture at Dell that is challenging and encourages constant growth, I have always sought out experiences that would force me to learn and grow. I credit my rapid recovery from my brain injury in large part

---

6. McGonigal, Jane. "The Game That Can Give You 10 Extra Years of Life." , TED, June 2012. Web. 27 June 2016.

HEAD FIRST

to these experiences. The neuropsychologist I worked with during my recovery was amazed that I had recovered from a GCS of 3 when I arrived at the hospital in Denver. She explained that 80% of the people with a GCS of 3 don't even survive. And of those who do, few recover at the speed or to the extent that I did. She explained that there are three factors that determine how a patient recovers from a brain injury: 1) no alcohol or drug abuse, 2) a strong support system surrounding the patient, and 3) the structure and chemistry of the brain they started with. I am lucky enough not to have a problem with drugs and alcohol. I also have the benefit of a fantastic support system. I humbly submit that I was intelligent prior to the accident, and because of my work at Dell where I was constantly learning in new challenging roles every couple years, I had trained my brain to be continuously learning and receptive to absorbing new information. The chemistry in my brain supported new neuron connection growth and enabled me to quickly recover from the deficits that showed up from my brain injury.

This is an example of neuroplasticity, which I introduced earlier. I learned about this scientific principle when I arrived home four weeks after the accident. I had asked myself, "Am I going to recover from my brain injury?" I was happy to learn from my neuropsychologist that the answer was yes, if I put in the work, I would heal my brain. That work simply meant challenging the areas of my mind where I had a deficit. By working on these weak spots, I was exercising the parts of my brain that were damaged. Each time I exercised this function, my brain would heal a little by growing new neuron connections and strengthening existing ones. As I started asking my brain to get better at memory recall, it built up the part of the brain that is used for memory recall. As I asked it to get better at logic puzzles, it built up the part

132

of the brain needed for performing logic puzzles.

No matter how old you are, your brain is constantly adapting and creating new neural pathways.[7] All you must do to build new neuron connections or strengthen existing ones is to put focused effort into it. It is the same concept at work when practicing a sport or a skill. Some people refer to it as muscle memory—the more you practice a skill, the better you get at it, the less you have to consciously think about it, and the more automatic it becomes. But it's not muscle memory; it's your brain building and strengthening the connections used for the skill. This is why I play better golf when I spend more time on the practice range. There is scientific proof of what's happening. One example of this is in a study of violinists where scientists studied their brains with MRI scans and found that the part of their brains dedicated to the left hand are larger than the right hand.[8] Then there is the famous study of London cab drivers that showed how the part of their brain dedicated to spatial maps is larger.[9] Both of these examples are because they used that part of their brain more, it developed more and became more capable. What this means for anyone with a brain injury is that science shows that your brain will continue to recover as long as you work at it. There isn't a time limit.

Neuroplasticity is great news for anyone who wants to become more positive. No matter where you are on the positivity scale now, if you practice, you will change the structure of your brain. By practicing positivity on a regular basis, you will increase the positivity circuits in your brain. In the last chapter I suggest establishing a positivity practice where you dedicate time to it each day.

---

7. "What Is Brain Plasticity?" *BrainHQ from Posit Science.* N.p., 15 July 2015. Web. 27 June 2016.

8. Assessment of sensorimotor cortical representation asymmetries and motor skills in violin players, European Journal of Neuroscience, 2007 Dec;26(11):3291-302, Schwenkreis P1, El Tom S, Ragert P, Pleger B, Tegenthoff M, Dinse HR.

9. London taxi drivers and bus drivers: a structural MRI and neuropsychological analysis., Maguire EA, Woollett K, Spiers HJ., Hippocampus. 2006;16(12):1091-101.

In the book, *The Happiness Advantage*, Shawn Achor refers to studies that demonstrate how a gratitude journal kept for seven days made people happier and less depressed, and that the benefits lingered for months. A more recent study used MRI scans and showed that gratitude expression made a differences in neural activity as much as three months later.[10]

Imagine a fishing bobber sitting in the water − this represents your current mindset. If your bobber is floating on the surface, you are in a positive mindset. If your bobber has been pulled underwater, you are in a negative mindset. Now, think of the size of your bobber as your positivity potential. When your bobber gets pulled underwater, and you go into a negative mindset, how much buoyancy force does your bobber have to overcome and pull it back to the surface? *How good is my bobber at staying on the surface when something is trying to pull it down? What is the force or potential it has to return me to a positive mindset?*

When you are facing difficult situations it is easy to get pulled down into negativity—pessimism, sadness, anger —and if you don't have enough resiliency in the forms I described earlier, it can be hard to pull yourself back to the surface. If you have been building up your positivity, then you will have a better chance of returning to a positive mindset and overcoming the challenges.

I was lucky in that when I had my accident, my bobber had a strong positivity potential and kept returning me to the surface despite the setbacks that tried to pull me down. When something went wrong in my recovery and I had a setback like the embolism that sent me back to the ICU, I had enough reserves to restore my positive attitude by the next day. When my pace of recovery slowed and it became

10. Kini, Prathik, Joel Wong, Sydney Mcinnis, Nicole Gabana, and Joshua W. Brown. "The Effects of Gratitude Expression on Neural Activity." NeuroImage 128 (2016): 1-10.

more mentally challenging, I overcame that frustration and found the motivation to continue with the hard work.

But, don't be disheartened if you think your bobber doesn't have much positivity potential. Through neuroplasticity, you can increase the buoyancy force of your bobber. Building up your positivity potential can happen at any time and at any stage in your life. By practicing the exercises I've described in this book you can boost your positivity and increase your bobber's potential so that when you inevitably experience a challenge, you can overcome it.

Sometimes what pulls our bobber underwater isn't necessarily a bad thing in and of itself; it represents an obstacle or a challenge, but also a chance to learn and grow. Maybe you have a fish on the line—a goal or an opportunity that is difficult to achieve—and you are being pulled down by a setback or feeling overwhelmed or doubting yourself. However, by having that bobber full of potential, you can pull yourself and that fish back to the surface and find the path to realizing your dream.

Additionally, setting your positive mindset—getting your bobber on the surface—before an important event in your life will make a major difference in your performance and your chance of success at the event. It works for any situation, whether it's a presentation or meeting at work, a crucial conversation with someone you care for, or in a sporting competition. There are several scientific studies that have shown a correlation between having a positive mindset going into the event and the outcome of the event.

Obviously, if you are in the middle of a setback, it's not useful to look at your situation and say, "I should have done _____ ," because that is only going to bring up more negativity. If you are neck-deep in a crisis, the way to get your bobber to the surface is to start by finding a positive thing in your situation and focusing on it. You'll be surprised by how your spirits and your mindset begin to rise.

If you happen to be in a good place and your bobber is resting on the surface right now, take the time to strengthen your positivity circuits in your brain and increase the buoyancy potential of your bobber. Then, when your bobber is pulled under, your positivity potential will be more capable of bringing you back to the surface, and you will be better equipped to not only overcome, but also to learn and grow from the setback or event that brought you down.

Like I said earlier, working on your positivity is like fitness for your attitude. Just like being physically fit, you get the benefits of increased energy, and you feel better overall. In addition, if you ever get into a health crisis, that fitness will help you recover. Not only do you get the benefit of better outcomes in the moments when you are in a positive mindset, but if you ever find yourself facing a challenge or a setback, you will have that attitude fitness built up to help you overcome it. What I call your attitude fitness or the buoyancy of your bobber is what psychologists call a 'positivity offset.' It's what counteracts the negativity bias that is natural in our brains.

POSITIVITY PRINCIPLE #8
EMBRACE GROWING PAINS AND LEARN FROM YOUR STRUGGLES

Building the potential of your positivity is straightforward: practice positivity, and you will grow the positivity circuits in your brain. You can do this in a number of different ways. One is to make a list of things that put you in a positive mindset. These things will be different for everyone, but I'll get you started by sharing what works for me.

Things that make me happy:

1) Investing in close personal relationships

2) Learning something new

3) Solving challenges or problems

4) Accomplishing goals

5) Enjoying nature

6) Helping or giving to others

Activities that put me in a positive mindset:

1) Giving someone a genuine compliment – This is most effective in person, though a phone call or text, but a post on a social media site will also work. Doing this boosts my positivity and how I feel about myself, not to mention how it will make the other person feel.

2) Exercising – Any exercise works for me. It can be something vigorous like running, or something a little more passive like yoga.

3) Standing or sitting in a confident posture for three minutes – It seems strange, but I can feel the difference in my positivity as I am doing this. I am amazed by how well it works for infusing positive feelings and assurance in my purpose. There is a great TED talk on this topic.[11]

4) Reciting goals or intentions – Reciting my life intentions each morning.

5) Going outside – I love the outdoors, so going outside puts me into a positive mindset. Finding a space that is quiet and calm-

11. Cuddy, Amy. "Your Body Language Shapes Who You Are." *www.TED.com*. TED, June 2012. Web. 28 June 2016

ing helps me get centered and focused for what lies ahead.

6) Looking at pictures of my loved ones – Keeping these important people in front of me helps me remember why I do what I do and what matters most to me.

7) Visualizing my goals – I have my own list of intentions posted, and I look at them or recite them nearly every day. I've set my screen saver to show me pictures of Yosemite—the start of the John Muir trail.

These activities are the tools I use to build my positivity potential that helps me when I experience a challenge or a setback. Although it may not be easy at the time, understanding that what pulls you down is an opportunity to learn and grow. Sometimes those things that seem like misfortunes pulling you below the surface may actually be a means for going deep to retrieve great things waiting for you below the surface.

From my own experience you can see how my accident is one of those things that dragged my bobber down, and my work to recover brought me back up. But what makes that time below the surface valuable is that I learned so much about myself and about positivity from this experience, and it opened me up to a world of opportunities I wouldn't have had otherwise. Had I not had this accident, I probably never would have begun speaking about positivity, and I definitely wouldn't have written this book.

Looking back, I had therapists who constantly kept tabs on my emotional state, and though I never experienced any form of depression or PTSD, I think part of my ability to remain positive was due to the fact that I could see continual progress.

I am often asked if I fully recovered. I didn't, and I have a few minor deficits. I have a slightly reduced range of motion in my arm and back, minor floaters in my left eye, a little hearing loss at high frequencies in my left ear, my voice is a little different, I have a 10% reduction in lung capacity, and I am one inch shorter. But mentally I've fully recovered, and I have no chronic pain. Am I really going to complain that my left eye still has a little fuzziness, or that I have some slight hearing loss when I still get to experience life? Even though I did not recover to 100% in all areas, and I do get reminded of my deficits at times, each time I experience the limitation, I don't get upset about what I can't do. Instead, it serves as a reminder that I am really lucky to be here.

Overall, I am stronger as a result of the accident. Although I'm not completely physically recovered, some areas like my positivity are much stronger, and I'm grateful to have recovered as I have. Gratitude has been my key to experiencing Post Traumatic Growth. If I can experience that in this situation, it's possible for you to embrace your growing pains and learn from your struggles too.

POSITIVITY IN PRACTICE

Use the section on the following page to document your list of what makes you happy. What do you enjoy doing? What gives you energy? When you are saying to yourself at the end of an activity or event, *That was Awesome! I loved that!* you have a good indicator of what should go on this list. When that happens, ask yourself, *What happened that made it awesome? What specifically gave me that feeling?*

These are the things that make me happy. I want more of the following in my life:

* _____
* _____
* _____
* _____
* _____
* _____
* _____

What are the activities you are willing to do to put yourself into a positive mindset?

* _____
* _____
* _____
* _____
* _____
* _____
* _____

Put these lists in a location where you will see them each day. I have mine posted where I get dressed each morning. It's awesome when I start my day looking at them and thinking, *I'm gonna get me some of that today!*

CONCLUSION
My Alive Day
Celebrate the Little Things

On March 9, 2015 I celebrated my first "Alive Day"—the one-year anniversary of my skiing accident. We had a nice dinner at home with my extended family in Austin. We didn't do anything extravagant, just ten of us around the table enjoying each other's company. Deanna baked a cake and wrote "Life is Good" on it. All I could say was, "I'm here! It's great to be here; it sure beats being dead!" Everyone agreed, retold stories about their memories of the accident day—where they were when they heard the news, and funny things that happened throughout my recovery.

As I was getting ready for bed that night, I was looking at my keepsakes on my dresser when I heard a voice in my head. I believe it was God's voice. It was the same voice that, about a year prior, told me, "Steve, if you want to live and see your kids again, you will need your lungs. If you want your lungs, you are going to have to fight for them." I credit that message and God with saving my life at that time. It's a voice I have heard three times in my life, and I've learned to listen to it.

This time the voice asked me a question: "Steve, you lived a bonus year. What did you do with it?" I was surprised by the question, and I stood there dumbfounded for a minute, trying to think of something important.

All I could come up with was, "I healed." My recovery had been miraculous, and it did require a great deal of work and energy.

The voice replied, "Okay. That was good."

I relaxed a little.

Then the voice added, "You aren't going to be able to say that again next year. What are you going to do with your next bonus year?"

Ugh. I had no idea what to say. I struggled to come up with an answer I thought would satisfy.

Finally, I answered, "I'm going to tell my story."

There was silence for a few moments, and the voice replied, "That will work," and it was gone.

Just thinking about it again now sends shivers down my spine. I was relieved I had come up with a satisfying answer, but I had no idea what telling my story actually meant. I had no idea who I should tell, what I would say, or how I should go about it.

The next day, I went to work at Dell with this thought of telling my story as a new personal mission for the year. Later that day, I saw a note from our talent development team about leadership training seminars they host for the organization. I thought, *There's a perfect place to start. But how is a story about a skiing accident related to work or leadership?* That was when I realized that my story isn't about my accident at all. It is about my recovery and overcoming obstacles. It is about attitude and positivity, which provides the foundation of leadership.

I spoke to the team that organized the talent development events, they thought it would be a great story to tell, and a few weeks later, I gave my first presentation to an audience of 250 people.

I received an overwhelming response. So many people found my story inspiring and relevant to their lives. It was an incredibly encouraging day, and I realized that this was a story worth telling.

Over the course of the next year, I told the story over twenty times to thousands of people inside and outside of Dell with similar responses from the audience. When I hear back from someone in the audience that my story changed their life, it fulfills and inspires me. About halfway through my second bonus year, after sharing the story several times and getting the same reactions, I made the decision to write this book. My goal is simply to share what I have learned with as many people as I can. As I've recounted the story to various audiences at large company settings, conferences, university classrooms, religious settings, and as a TED talk, I've realized that this story is relevant to everyone.

I'm hopeful that on my second Alive Day, if God's voice returns to me, that I will hear satisfaction in that voice for what I've accomplished in my second bonus year. I'm not sure what I'll say about my intentions for my third bonus year, but I expect it will still be to spread this message to as many people as possible. The more people who hear this message, the better the world will be. I'm thrilled to have a role to play in making the world a better place. I believe this is partly why God brought me back.

One of the common questions I get when I tell my story is, "Will you ever ski again?" My answer is, "Of course!" And, I find it fitting that I am working on this last chapter while in Deer Valley, Utah on my first ski trip since the accident. Everyone, including me, has been understandably anxious about my getting back on skis, and now that I am here, a little less than two years after the accident, I find it a little surreal. I was more anxious than I anticipated. When I rented my skis, I told the technician what had happened the last time I was on the slopes and showed him a picture of the helmet. He checked the settings on the ski bindings three times, and I checked them a fourth!

That night it snowed a couple inches. The conditions the next day were cold, but otherwise perfect. When I woke up to find tons of base, fresh powder, I became even more anxious and ready to go.

We got to the base of Deer Valley resort, and everyone went their separate ways to get their boots on, pull skis from storage, and get lift tickets. I put my boots on, got my lift ticket, and carried my skis and poles up the small incline just outside the lift entrance. I laid the skis on the snow to put them on and stared at them. I paused for a moment and asked myself, *Are you really doing this?*

As I stepped into the bindings and heard the click affirming that the skis were attached to my boots, I could feel my pulse quicken. I looked up at the people around me, and no one seemed to notice. I was just another skier getting ready for a run, just like them. They had no idea how special that moment was for me.

I stared down at my skis for a minute. I stomped them—bouncing the front and back of the skis on the snow to make sure the bindings wouldn't release. I took a picture of my boots and the skis. It felt a little silly taking the picture, but I wanted to capture and remember that moment.

The first day of skiing was great. The second day was great. The third and final day was going great. My companions all quit after lunch on the third day, but I wasn't done yet. I wanted to get the most out of my last day, so I stayed on the slopes. As I skied a few more blue groomed runs, I could hear the black runs calling me. I stared at them as I went up the lift alone, and I just couldn't resist, so I spent the rest of the afternoon on the black bump runs having a ball.

As I left the last run that day, near the lift closing time, I thought, *I did it! I skied again!* There were no flashbacks, no accidents. I realized that this was the last milestone in my recovery. That long arduous chapter in my life was over.

I have learned a lot about myself in the last two years of recovery, and I have learned a lot about positivity. I have experienced dramatic personal growth, and my perspective on life has changed in three important ways:

1) I value my time much more than ever before.
2) I am more purposeful with how I spend my time.
3) I enjoy everyday moments much more.

My hope is that this book has provided you with a bit of inspiration and the tools to act on that inspiration to change the course of your day and, ultimately your life. If I've done that, then I've accomplished my goal. Please share this story with someone you love. Give them this book. It will help me with my goal of getting this message to as many people around the world as possible. Together we can make the world a more positive place and the people around us much happier.

The key lessons I hope you take away from this story are:

1) A positive attitude will lead to better outcomes.
2) You can train your brain to be more positive.
3) There are simple, practical things you can do to become more positive, and get those better outcomes in your life.

The best time to plant a tree is 20 years ago.
The second best time is now.
—Chinese Proverb

Now it's up to you. Take your first step on your positivity journey. Pick one of the principles of this book to apply to your life. Find a situation in your life where you can benefit from some positivity and move from *"Why me?"* to *"What now?"*

ACKNOWLEDGMENTS

First and foremost, I want to acknowledge my wife, Deanna, for saving my life with her tireless support and amazing attitude during my recovery. Her incredible strength and positivity enabled her to endure this incredibly stressful time and lead me through it. I would not have survived without her. I love you, Deanna.

My children, Ryan and Katie, who were amazing during my recovery. They were strong, encouraging, and played an important role helping me recover. Their presence in my life and the love we share is one of the motivators for me to navigate all the hard work and misery of my recovery.

Peter Markes for saving me on the mountain, keeping it together with Deanna in those early days, and helping with our children while Deanna and I stayed in Denver.

Dana Markes for taking care of our families during those first few days, helping Deanna and me in the hospital that first week, caring for our children while Deanna and I remained in Denver, and for the support over the next several months.

My mother, brother, sister, and mother-in-law, Jimbo and Jamie Cotton, Jeff and Missy Hillhouse for traveling to visit me and provide their love and support.

Dr. Michael Desaloms, a family friend and neurosurgeon who provided valuable advice to Deanna to help her with my medical decisions.

Ned Murphy and Jay Schroeder for driving to Denver in an RV and bringing Deanna and me home to Austin.

All the family, friends, and coworkers who prayed for me, sent cards, flowers, gifts, well wishes, support, and positive energy to me. I remain humbled by the number of people that reached out during this difficult time.

Ryan's Westwood High School Lacrosse team, coaches, and parents for their prayers and support.

All the neighborhood friends who supported and helped me and my family with visits, meals, driving, domestic help, etc.

Steve Lalla, Jeff Clarke, and everyone at Dell who supported me throughout the ordeal, my recovery, and my return to full time work.

Julie Gross for sending Henrietta!

The Breckenridge Ski Patrol who made the critical first decisions and quickly got me down the mountain and into the care of the Breckenridge medical staff.

The doctors, nurses, and staff at the Breckenridge Hospital at the base of the mountain including Dr. Bernard Riberdy.

The crew and nurses on Flight for Life® helicopter, Pilot Loren Courtney, Kevin Kelble, (EMT-P), and David Repsher (nurse).

The doctors, nurses, and staff at St. Anthony's hospital in Denver that saved my life in Trauma 10 surgery including the primary surgeon Dr. Fred Seale, Dr. John Hudson, Dr. Heit, Jeffery Huber, P.A., Schermerhorn, P.A., Allison Bricker, R.N., Keith Roussel, R.N, Rae (OR RN), Jen (OR RN), Jamie (ICU RN), Eric (ICU RN), Jason Zukosky (OR specialist), Andrew (OR Tech), Youri (Phlebotomist), Doug (Radiology Tech), Sonya (Recorder), Karen Melliar Smith (Ansethisia CRNA).

Other doctors, nurses, and staff at St. Anthony's Hospital who participated in my care, Dr. Philip Yarnell, Dr. Douglas Wong, Dr. Jesse Bolton, Dr. Thomas Puschak, Dr. Michael Tralla, Dr. Mathew Stewart Cushing, Dr. Clinton Anderson, Dr. Jeffery Guay, Dr. Christopher Leoni, Dr. Earl Woolley, Dr. Patrick Moore, Dr. Maruyama, Dr. Jennifer Jeans, Dr. Carmen Cojanu, Dr. Gregory Hickey, Dr. Charles Norton, Dr. Robert Leibold, Dr. Jeffrey Moulton, Dr. Steven Ross, Dr. Trent Paradis, Dr. Richard Stewart, Dr. Joshua Bryant, Dr. Joseph Burchenal, Dr. John Svinarich, Sony Burgers Silleck, P. A.,

Jody Benjamin Kramer, P. A., Lindsey Henninger, P.A, Nurse Eric, Allison, Kate, Jamie, Kathy, Toni, Brad, therapists Melissa, Anna, and Cynthia.

I would also like to acknowledge the numerous therapists, nurses, & other staff members who helped me during my stay at St. Anthony's hospital. Unfortunately, I do not have all the names of everyone who helped me. The harp player and the cello player who came into my ICU room and played beautiful music to my wife and me. Also, the several therapy dogs that came by my hospital room.

The doctors, nurses, and staff at St. David's inpatient and outpatient rehab and follow-up Doctors inside and outside the St. David's system: Dr. Everett Heinze, my primary doctor at St. David's Inpatient rehab. Also Dr. Frederick Fung, Dr. Joshua Fox, Dr. Anant Patel, Dr. Thomas Chandler, Dr. Hicks, Dr. Dan Peterson, Dr. Andrew Lee (Neuro-Ophthalmology) Methodist Hospital in Houston), and Jenny Benevides RN.

The therapists and staff at Rehab without Walls: Mollie Miller, Erika Aguilar, Hannah Friesen, Gail Wagner, Shannon Grethel Psy.D., and Lisa Wright.

Dr. Parvis Kavoussi for my men's health—I was diagnosed with low testosterone a few years prior to the accident, and he had placed me on slow release testosterone pellets prior to the accident that kept my levels in a normal range during my recovery. Having a steady, normal level of testosterone was an important factor in both my attitude and my rate of healing.

Dr. Stephanie Shaw at Texas Diabetes and Endochrinology for treating me for hypothyroidism. Having stable thyroid hormone levels also helped my energy and attitude during my recovery.

Dr. Mike Bhatt, my chiropractor for helping me regain nearly full range of motion in my neck and back. Also, his Swingbak foam roller is awesome.

Ken Moench, the massage therapist at Therapy Central in Austin.

Casey Crevelone, my physical trainer at Lifetime Fitness in Austin before and after the accident.

Finally, I would like to thank the team at The Fedd Agency and

Cara Highsmith for their help in making this book a reality.

I'm sure I will remember someone who deserves credit as soon as this goes to print. Whomever it is that I forgot to mention here, thank you.

ABOUT THE AUTHOR

Steve Lawton holds a BS and MS degree in Mechanical Engineering from Texas A&M University, as well as an MBA from St. Edwards University. He has twenty-seven years of experience in roles from engineering in the Astronaut Office at NASA to an executive at Dell.

Steve enjoys speaking and sharing what he has learned about positive leadership from his career and his experience recovering from a near fatal skiing injury in March 2014. Through his unique experiences, Steve has molded his messages and insights about how to create a positive mindset, lead with positivity, and achieve better outcomes for individuals and organizations.

Steve and his wife of twenty-six years, Deanna, have two teenage children, and they have grown quite fond of them.

@leadpositivity

www.stevehlawton.com